The Andrew R. Cecil Lectures on Moral Values in a Free Society

established by

The University of Texas at Dallas

Volume V

THE CITIZEN AND HIS GOVERNMENT

The Citizen and His Government

ADLAI E. STEVENSON
ANDREW R. CECIL
RICHARD JOHN NEUHAUS
ROBERT L. PAYTON
PETER J. STANLIS
RICHARD YOUNG

With an Introduction by
ANDREW R. CECIL

Edited by
W. LAWSON TAITTE
The University of Texas at Dallas
1984

Library of Congress Catalog Card Number 83–50618
International Standard Book Number 0-292-71104-2

Distributed by the University of Texas Press,
Box 7819, Austin, Texas 78712

FOREWORD

The week of November 14, 1983, marked the fifth series of the Andrew R. Cecil Lectures on Moral Values in a Free Society at The University of Texas at Dallas. Since it was estasblished in 1979, this annual series has become an important tradition of the University. Each year scholars and leaders of national prominence share with the academic community and the public their most carefully considered reflections concerning the moral values that our country was built on. In providing this forum, the University is fulfilling its responsibility to see that these values are understood and preserved. Reaching beyond merely practical concerns, this program offers an opportunity for analysis and debate of the moral basis of a free society.

The lectures are named for Dr. Andrew R. Cecil, the University's Distinguished Scholar in Residence and the Chancellor Emeritus of The Southwestern Legal Foundation. When he served as President of the Foundation, his leadership of that institution gained him the highest respect in educational and legal circles throughout the United States. When he became Chancellor Emeritus of the Foundation, Dr. Cecil consented to serve as Distinguished Scholar in Residence at The University of Texas at Dallas. The Lectures on Moral Values in a Free Society are aptly named for a man who, throughout his career, has consistently been concerned with the moral verities, always stressing a faith in the dignity and worth of every individual.

The 1983 lectures were organized around the topic "The Citizen and His Government." Dr. Cecil was joined by a former United States Senator, a theologian, a foundation president, a professor, and a lawyer. Each of the lecturers is distinguished professionally, but—more importantly—each has also demonstrated a profound understanding of the moral imperatives of the relationship between individuals and the governance of this society. We are most grateful to Messrs. Stevenson, Cecil, Neuhaus, Payton, Stanlis, and Young for their willingness to share their ideas and for the thoughtful lectures that are preserved in this volume.

U.T. Dallas extends its appreciation to all those who have helped make the lectures an important part of the life of the University, especially to the supporters of the Cecil Lectures. Through their contributions, these donors enable us to continue this important educational endeavor and to publish the lectures, thus ensuring a wide and permanent audience for the ideas they present.

I am confident that all those who read the lectures published in this fifth volume of the Andrew R. Cecil Lectures, *The Citizen and His Government,* will be stimulated to give additional thought to the vital issues discussed.

ROBERT H. RUTFORD, President
The University of Texas at Dallas
January 1984
Dallas, Texas

CONTENTS

Foreword 7
   Andrew R. Cecil

Introduction 11
   Andrew R. Cecil

The Ethics of National Elections:
   The Presidency 27
   Adlai E. Stevenson

Due Process of Law:
   The Bulwark of a Free Society 45
   Andrew R. Cecil

Demoracy, Economics, and Radical
   Pluralism 97
   Richard John Neuhaus

Philanthropy as a Right 123
   Robert L. Payton

Constitutional Liberty in Western Civilization:
   The American Republic 145
   Peter J. Stanlis

World Perspectives in International Law:
   Moral Values in Relations Across
   National Boundaries 221
   Richard Young

INTRODUCTION

by Andrew R. Cecil

To Greece we attribute the first attempt to construct the prototype of the modern State—the city-state—and the creation of political science, a science aimed at finding the avenues leading toward order in a civilized society. The true mark of a city-state (for which the Greeks had one word—"polis") was its economic and political independence. The thoughts of Greek philosophers centered around the city-state, and the allegiance and devotion of the ancient Greeks to the "polis" made their city the precursor of the State as known in our time.

The term "democracy" was originated in Greece to describe a government where people participate in directing the affairs of the State and in making its laws. While Sparta was a militarized society, democracy reached its fullest expression in ancient Athens. Obviously democracy had its shortcomings in practice. For Plato, the participation of the masses in government, which in extreme form becomes mob-rule, and the principles advocated by democracy, which include equality of rights and freedom of speech, were only sources of evil. Plato rejected democracy completely, while Aristotle accepted it as a lesser evil.

Plato's ideal city-state is a three-class society. The classification is based on functions to be performed. The guardians represent the supreme authority of government; endowed with wisdom and courage, they rule and protect the State. Their orders are carried out by the auxiliary protectors, who are employed by the government in various ways as members of the civil service and the military or police force. Like the guardians, the auxiliary protectors possess the combination of courage and gentleness—they should be ruthless toward external foes and gentle with their own people. The third class represents the rest of the population, and its members serve the economic needs of the community.

This classification based on function does not correspond to the contemporary concept of social classes. All citizens in the Platonic State have a common origin. There is a reliance on heredity in the choice of guardians and auxiliaries, but in order to assure for the State the services of the best-qualified men, promotion of exceptional children from the third class to a higher grade and relegation of unsuitable children from the upper classes to a lower grade is expected.

Aristotle defines a citizen as "one who is capable of ruling and being ruled in turn," but more in harmony with the facts of Greek history is his definition describing a citizen as "one who has part in judicial decisions, and in holding office." The Greeks called the rule of the freeman exercised by each individual citizen through the assembly and the law courts democracy. Under pure democracy the mere fact of "free birth" was sufficient to establish a claim to these offices that directed the administration of the State.

Such pure democracy did not exist in Greece. There was always an aristocratic or oligarchic basis for representation in the State. The masses could only claim the power of criticism and judgment of the government's policies and conduct. Where we have mob-rule, stated Aristotle, we have demagogues: "For in cities governed democratically, but also legally, there are no demagogues; the best among the citizens take the lead." He warned that when "demagogues come into play" democracy turns into tyranny.

Plato was an Athenian aristocrat and a puritan. Aristotle, his pupil, was the son of a physician, a philosopher, and a student of marine biology. As a middle-class professional man, he recognized the importance of the man in the street. He wished to combine aristocracy, the essence of which is "distribution of offices according to goodness," with the will of the majority, which in a democracy should prevail. He saw good government in cities with a large middle class, which has a "great steadying influence and checks the opposing extremes" of the rich and the poor.

While Plato's guardians, after thirty years of training and apprenticeship, were to hold office for life, the democratic constitutions of the States in fact called for service in government for a limited time only. This constitutional requirement raised, according to Aristotle, the questions of the continuity of government and of the contractual obligations between the city or the old government and the new government.

Greece remained in a condition of perpetual

change, and with each change of the constitution a shift took place in the balance of power. The principles of political compromise and of mutual concessions which frequently applied in the history of Rome were not a feature of most of the Greek city-states. In early Rome, the basis of political origanization was the clan *(gens)*. The patricians were the legitimate sons in the families belonging to the *gentes* recognized by the State. Only the particians had full rights of citizenhsip. Among the most important political privileges were the right to vote and the right to hold office. In exceptional cases, the most prominent families in the conquered countries were admitted among the *gentes* and to the full rights of citizenship enjoyed by the patricians.

Attached to the *gentes* were hereditary dependents known as *clientes,* comprised of those who came to Rome after the conquest of their native land or of strangers who came to Rome attracted by the possibility of improving their condition, or of freedmen. *Clientes* as a rule enjoyed the privileges of their *patroni* in return for performance of certain duties they owed their patrons, who represented him before the law. Released gradually from their duties, *clientes* and newcomers, who did not attach themselves to the representatives of prominent Roman families, formed a second class known as the *plebs,* which lacked organization, had no part in the management of Rome's affairs, and was denied the civil rights and political privileges of the patricians.

This class discrimination and prejudice in favor of patricians became a source of serious conflicts. The able-bodied plebeians who served in the army and participated in the military expansion of Rome demanded a voice in government. Through compromises and political concessions, the plebeians under the empire made great constitutional gains that ended the patricio-plebeian struggle.

The accumulation of wealth in the hand of a few almost eliminated the independent middle class. Although under the Empire citizenship meant practically the same for patricians and plebeians, there came forth gradually a second class that comprised those who were outside the privileged classes. This class, known as "plebs"—the term used also under the Republic—was essentially without political rights, but its members could rise into higher orders by acquiring a fortune required by these higher orders (senatorial and equestrian). The class of the plebeians which evolved under the Empire differed essentially, therefore, from the class of the plebeians that existed under the early Republic.

In the medieval ages, the great mass of the less fortunate were bound to service on land in return for the protection their landlords could provide them. In the feudal structure, where ownership of land became a system of government, we may find the seeds of the idea of a contract binding the rulers and the people and involving mutual duties. This idea was an important development in the philosophy of democracy.

In the 17th century, Baruch Spinoza (born in 1632)—considered by many the greatest modern philosopher—formulated the political philosophy of democracy that became the main source of the stream of thought that culminated in Jean-Jacques

Rousseau, the French philosopher, and his exposition of the theory of the social contact(*Contrat Social* 1762). Individuals, according to Rousseau, surrender their power over themselves to the people as a whole, thus creating popular, infallible sovereignty functioning through the power of majority decisions—representing the general will.

In England, the leader of the constitution's development leading toward increased power of the people by parliamentary means was John Locke. In *Two Treatises of Government* (1690), Locke expounded the idea of democracy derived from the social contract and based on natural law. The social contract, maintains Locke, vests sovereignty in the people, who have the right and the obligation to withdraw their support of a government that does not comply with the popular will. The term "consent of the governed" has, therefore, a different meaning than it had in Greece under class rule, or in Rome where the *ius civile* of the Romans was the privilege of the Roman citizen, or in the medieval process of benevolent despotism.

The writers of the American Constitution drew heavily on the theory of law and government expounded by John Locke by weaving into the very fabric of its legal order the concepts of Natural Law and Natural Right. Our idea of government, republic in form, implies a right on the part of its citizens to assemble peaceably for consultation and to petition the government for redress of grievances and a right to vote. The Nineteenth Amendment to the Constitution states, "The right of citizens of the United States to vote shall not be abridged by the United

States or by any State on account of sex." After 124 years, the election of Senators by the legislatures of the individual states was superseded by direct elections by the people upon the adoption (May 31, 1913) of the Seventeenth Amendment. With federalized citizenship the right to vote is a federal constitutional right.

The importance of voting for a free, responsible, statesmanlike government was described in a colorful way by the Court of Appeals of Kentucky (in the case of *Illinois Central Railroad Co. v. Commonwealth,* to which I refer in the chapter on "Due Process of Law"):

> "The woman with the sun bonnet and the checkered apron who trudges off of the mountain side in Leslie County and walks down the creek a mile to cast her vote—she is an American queen in calico, but her only pay for voting is the satisfaction of knowing that Columbia, by God's help and hers, shall continue as the gem of the mighty ocean. Let no man cease to thank his God as he looks in at the open door of his voting place, as he realizes that here his quantity, though cast in overalls, is exactly the same as the quantity of the President of the United States. There is a satisfaction and privilege in voting in a free country that cannot be measured in dollars and cents."

Former Senator Adlai E. Stevenson, in his lecture "The Ethics of National Elections: The Presidency," stresses that the free political processes of the United States have served this nation well. He laments the excessively skeptical attitude with which the public has come to view political life. Such an attitude undermines confidence in our political system. While it is true that men and systems are imperfect and that abuses of trust are bound to occur, Senator Stevenson argues that excessive distrust of the individuals involved in government and a consequent attempt to limit their powers causes a deterioration in our political life.

Senator Stevenson's remedy for the problems of government is not a rush to make new laws. He seeks, rather, a new commitment by individuals with vision who will lead this country in new directions—individuals who have "the courage to be right." He believes that the relationship of a citizen and his government will work out most satisfactorily when the citizen assumes responsibility for taking an active part in the life of his country, thus helping to make the decisions which will affect his life and those of his fellow citizens.

The structures and processes of our governmental system rest on the realization that limits on its power were wisely built into the system. Such limits do not call for an excessive distruct of government. *The Federalist,* described by Thomas Jefferson as "the best commentary on the principles of government which was ever written," in its emphasis on the role of government makes the following statement: "A good government implies two things: first, fidelity to the object of government, which is happiness of the people, secondly, a knowledge of the means by which the object can be obtained." *(Federalist 62).* One of the principal means of assuring the proper balance of our government is the right to "due process of law," which rests on the Fifth and Fourteenth Amendments.

Reinold Niebuhr wrote: "Man's capacity for justice makes democracy possible, but man's inclination to injustice makes democracy necessary." To paraphrase this statement, we may say that man's or government's inclination to injustice makes due process of law necessary. In my lecture on "Due Process of Law—The Bulwark of Democracy," I have tried to point out that the very nature of due process negates any concept of inflexible standards applicable to every imaginable situation. Its meaning and application will vary according to circumstances, although its purpose is always to insure fair and orderly administration of the laws to protect our fundamental rights against federal or state encroachment.

Although "due process" has never achieved a precise meaning, it serves as a means of social control by safeguarding us against the possibilities of executive, legislative, or military tyranny. Justice Louis D. Brandeis in his dissent in the *Olmstead* case explained: "Decency, security, and liberty alike demand that government officials shall be subjected to the same rules of conduct that are commands to the citizens. In a government of laws, evidence of the government will be imperiled if it fails to observe the law scrupulously. Our government is the potent, the omnipresent teacher. For good or ill, it teaches the whole people by example." (*Olmstead v. United States*, 277 U.S. 438, 485 [1928].)

The rules of conduct "that are commands to the citizens" call for a respect for the worth and dignity of one's fellowman and an appreciation of the imperatives of social justice. In the Book of the Covenant—handed down on Mount Sinai—we find God's concern for the widows, orphans, and strangers, for the poor, the weak, and the distressed. In this revelation, the Israelites are reminded that they "were strangers in the land of Egypt" and that their "wives shall be widows" and their "children fatherless" if they oppress orphans or widows. They are warned not to commit usury nor to take the poor's "raiment to pledge." God's concern extends to every action and to every person, and He gives asurance that when the oppressed "cries to me, I will hear, for I am compassionate." (Exodus 22:21-27.)

The Christian teaching also is to love one's neighbor. The prominent nineteenth-century Danish philosopher and theologian, Soren Kierkegaard, wrote, "If there are only two men, the other man is the neighbor; if there are millions, each one of these is the neighbor . . ." The distress and impoverishment of any single human being in the world is a challenge to his fellowman. The gifts of the Creator are man's inalienable rights, and God gives us the means by which all men may have an abundant life.

Commenting on theological virtues of faith, hope and charity, Thomas Aquinas explains: "Faith then and hope attain to God, inasmuch as the knowledge of truth, or the obtaining of good, comes to us of Him: but charity attains to God Himself, to rest in Him, not that anything may accrue to us of Him. And therefore charity is more excellent than faith or hope, and consequently than all other virtues."

In his address "Philanthropy as a Right," Robert L.

Payton distinguishes between two ways of expressing the love of one's fellowman of which Aquinas writes. The activity which we commonly call "charity" Mr. Payton likens to the relief aid citizens of one country extend to another; "philanthropy," on the other hand, more resembles developmental aid which helps others to help themselves. Mr. Payton traces the history of the two kinds of eleemosynary activity and reflects on the unique character of the American philanthropic system. Indeed, in many countries all charitable activity is outlawed.

The encouragement of private philanthropy is one of the great pillars of the freedoms of our country and one that it is taken too much for granted, Mr. Payton further argues. Since the great outpouring of philanthropic activity plays such a vital part in our nation's life, it should be studied much more closely and our citizens should be made much more aware of its scope and importance.

One of the great advantages of the enormous variety of charitable and philanthropic activity in our country is that it allows all citizens to decide for themselves which causes to support—creating, in effect, a "free market" of religious, educational, medical, and many other sorts of institutions which are at liberty to seek aid from individuals, businesses, and private foundations. One consequence of this system is the pluralistic nature of our society; certainly one of the strengths of this nation is that so many competing ideas and ideals exist side by side.

In his lecture "Democracy, Economics, and Radical Pluralism," however, Pastor Richard John Neuhaus suggests that the pluralistic character of our society can only go so far. If our society is to cohere, it must finally be founded on basic values on which all can agree. If there is not such a shared set of ideals and goals, then public discourse polarizes our society and paralyzes public harmonious action.

Pastor Neuhaus, by tracing the moral foundations of our society, points out that some moral presuppositions emanating from socialism permeate our moral discourse as a result of an exaggerated pluralism. He distinguishes between a belief in a moral responsibility for one's fellowman and the program offered by socialism for discharging that responsibility. In making this distinction, he calls for a reexamination of the moral values which underlie our social system in the light of the practical outcome of the experiments in socialism which our century has witnessed—experiments that have failed to promote individual liberty or even economic well-being. Only by examining our own social and economic system in the light of eternal moral values can a credible alternative to socialism and communism be articulated.

Certainly, over the years, we have seen a changing attitude about the role of government within our society and its economic life. Society is a product of man's social nature. His needs are the ultimate foundation of all government; his interest in creating a system of governmental authority is to keep it in the service of humanity and to prevent it from being turned against him. Over the last century, we can observe a trend of growing emphasis on governmental authority over many areas of the life of our society, especially economic ones. The accelerated governmental responsibility for social welfare programs and the dramatic growth in the extent of governmental interference in economic life that occurred within only seven decades are illustrated by the following excerpts from two messages by Chief Executives to Congress. The first came from President Grover Cleveland on February 16, 1887:

> "I do not believe that the power and duty of the General Government ought to be extended to the relief of individual suffering which is in no matter properly related to the public service or benefit. A prevalent tendency to disregard the limited mission of this power and duty should, I think, be steadfastly resisted, to the end that the lesson should be constantly enforced that though the people support the Government, the Government should not support the people."

The second message was sent by President Dwight D. Eisenhower on January 14, 1954:

> "The human problems of individual citizens are a proper and important concern of our Government. One such problem that faces every individual is the provision of economic security for his old age and economic security for his family in the event of his death. To help individuals provide for the security—to reduce both the fear and the incidence of destitution to the minimum—to promote the confidence of every individual in the future—these are proper aims of all levels of government, including the federal Government."

The great increase in the people's expectations of government, in the services provided by govern-

ment, and in the responsibilities which government
has assumed has increasingly made social man
political man. The history of civilized man has been
the preoccupation with the relationship of "political
man" to his government. Since ancient times, man
has sought to protect the individual citizen from the
encroachment of uncontrolled governmental
power—this search and the embodiment of these
values are enshrined in the thoughts and writings of
countless philosphers, theologians, lawgivers, and
legal instruments regulating the individual's rights
and restricting the power of the State.

Professor Peter J. Stanlis, in his address "Constitutional Liberty in Western Civilization: The
American Republic," goes back to the earliest of
these great traditions and traces the history of the
idea of constitutional liberty from ancient times to
the present. He sees the foundation of the American
republic as the culmination of an intellectual and
social process that had gone on for centuries—the
fulfillment of the ideas and dreams of many generations of men. In an imperfect world, the elaborate
safeguards of individual liberty built into our written
Constitution (and the moral values implicit in our
unwritten constitution) form the best system yet
devised by man for relating a citizen to his government. Professor Stanlis, however, expresses some
alarm that these safeguards have been eroded by the
gradual transformation of a republican form of government into a social democracy.

As our world is confronted daily with new social,
political, and economic changes, the responsibilities
of the citizen and his government become more and

more numerous and complex. Their task is to insure that the impact of the process that makes change imperative will result in the improvement of existing conditions. To ease international tensions and conflicts that have torn the globe for generations, the people of the world have to realize that they are partners in a great world partnership of nations in which every peace-loving nation wishes to determine its own life and institutions and to be assured of justice and fair dealing by the other partners.

Richard Young, in his lecture "World Perspectives in International Law: Moral Values in Relations Across National Boundaries," on the whole takes an optimistic view of the progress the world community of nations has made in the gradual process of agreeing to a body of international law. The interdependence of nations—scientifically, economically, and socially—becomes ever greater. Correspondingly, the legal ties which bind nations together grow ever more important. The efficacy of international law demands that nations accept its provisions and, even more important, its ideals. Mr. Young points out that many nations are gradually increasing their acceptance of the constraints of international law.

Many of the most remarkable cases of this willingness of nations to reach an accommodation with one another have gone relatively unnoticed, because they are not so dramatic as the expressions of international tension. Among those areas which Mr. Young discusses are new agreements affecting the law of outer space and the law of the sea. Although much progress has been made in these realms, much more remains to be accomplished, and Mr. Young emphasizes that such change is inevitably slow and careful. But progress must be made, for each human being is not only a citizen with responsibilities toward his own nation and its government but a citizen of the world as well, with universal obligations as well as rights.

In all the lectures in the 1983 Lectures on Moral Values in a Free Society, the theme is repeatedly emphasized that to insure the proper relationship between a citizen and his government each individual must assume his proper responsibility and all citizens must acknowledge that there are overarching moral values which bind them together and regulate their behavior.

The wide distribution of centers of power and the proper use of government are essential to provide the environment in which democratic freedom can flourish in the relations between the citizen and his government. We must face up to the issues involved both in freedom and in the abuse of freedom. In determining the citizen's responsibilities and the needs which will be satisfied by government, it is well to remember that God's unique design for man, unlike that for all other creatures, is the power to choose between good and evil. The consequences of our choice may lead to a fruitful existence or to agony and frustration.

THE ETHICS OF NATIONAL ELECTIONS: THE PRESIDENCY

by

Adlai E. Stevenson

Adlai E. Stevenson

After 16 years in elective office and a campaign for Governor of Illinois, Mr. Stevenson returned to the law firm of Mayer, Brown and Platt in January 1983. He maintains offices in Chicago and Washington, D.C. In addition to the practice of law, he lectures, operates a farm, and keeps his hands in politics.

Mr. Stevenson graduated from Harvard College in 1952. Following service as a tank platoon commander with the Marine Corps in Korea, he graduated from the Harvard Law School (1957) and clerked for a Justice of the Illinois Supreme Court. In 1958 he joined Mayer, Brown and Platt.

In the 1964 at-large election for the Illinois House of Representatives, he led all 236 candidates and later earned the "Best Legislator" award of the Independent Voters of Illinois. In 1966 he was elected Illinois State Treasurer. He made that office a national model, tripling earnings on state funds and keeping those funds at work in Illinois.

Mr. Stevenson was elected to the United States Senate by large margins in 1970 and 1974. In the Senate he warned of the coming energy crisis and began many of the efforts to formulate energy policy for the country. Mr. Stevenson then grappled with the economic implications of the energy crisis and declining U.S. competitiveness. His concerns included the international monetary and banking systems, industrial innovation, regulatory policy, and U.S. export policy. He recommended measures to improve the export competitiveness of the U.S. and its capacity for technological innovation. These measures include the Export Trading Company Act and the Stevenson-Wydler Technology Innovation Act. Mr. Stevenson also had the immediate responsibility for science and technology, including national space policy. He oversaw development of the space shuttle.

Mr. Stevenson led a major reorganization of the Senate in 1976-1977. He served as the first chairman of the Senate Select Committee on Ethics.

THE ETHICS OF NATIONAL ELECTIONS: THE PRESIDENCY

by Adlai E. Stevenson

It is said that policies of the United States have undergone a kind of sea change under President Reagan. The growth of the federal government was arrested. The country is being rearmed. Military force is now a ready means of serving national interests. But, if there is change, it is with little of the purpose that animates a people and exalts a nation to high endeavor.

Much of the "Reagan Revolution," the arms buildup, for example, proceeds in directions already established, though to extremes. The invasion of Grenada has antecedents in Southeast Asia, Cuba, and Tehran under other Presidents. Even symbols, the President in the Korean DMZ, are reminiscent of President Kennedy at the Berlin Wall, Mr. Bryzinski in the Khyber Pass. The realities are, as usual, at some variance with the images. The response of President Carter to the Russian invasion of Afghanistan was more punitive than the largely rhetorical responses of President Reagan to Russian excesses in Poland and Sakhalin. President Carter imposed the grain embargo; President Reagan lifted it. Some breaks with past policies, supply side economics, for example, may be short lived. After the election, when tax increases are not so imprudent, economic orthodoxy will resume.

What continues most consistently are the incongruities and inconsistencies of our policies. The process by which policy is made continues. By and large, that process produces outcomes, no matter who is President, that reflect little consistency—and less inspiration. Process governs—and process by itself has little purpose. We redouble defense efforts, as much from the momentum of this process as from purposes to be achieved by our weapons.

The process by which we, as a people, convert our values and opinions to our collective policies is politics. Politics, an Illinois clergyman suggested, is "applied religion." In practice the means by which the governed govern in the United States has always fallen short of the nation's purposes, let alone converting evangelical virtues to the nation's policies. We were left with an ambivalent attitude toward politics. Americans habitually revere the founders of their politics and deride its practitioners. The American politician, reviled in his lifetime, is often elevated to the rank of statesman at death. But we were not overly quarrelsome with our politics. After all, the nation came to span a continent and dominate the commerce of the world in little more than a century and a half. Our politics served our purposes well.

In recent years the healthy, historical skepticism toward politics has come close to cynicism. The young nation, poor but confident, built grand monuments to its politics in Washington. In its maturity, rich but less confident, works of marble on the Potomac are disparaged as another example of self-indulgence by politicians. Some politicians rail against the government of which they are a part, confirming and exploiting the skepticism. It is as if government had become a burden, a heavy object to get off our collective back, instead of the only means by which we achieve national purposes.

A prominent historian suggests that American politics ebbs and flows between the leadership of "realists" and "ideologues." In its finer moments the country is led by realists—men who understand the complexities of their time and deal with them realistically. Then the country falls back upon ideologues with simplistic but appealing ideas that give vent to public frustrations but often have little relevance to our condition. Expectations excited by simple ideas are then disappointed. But this explanation is simplistic.

In the last two decades the United States experienced social change which influenced politics. Minorities and women asserted their birthrights. Newfound rights of the individual to personal expression broke down social codes and challenged authority. The authority of school, church, and family, as well as government, was breaking down, too. Human reactions to events became more intuitive and emotional, less disciplined. It may not have been the expression of reason or ideology so much as emotion and personality and systemic change that determined political outcomes.

Out of all this change I sense a discontinuity in our history, a break in our politics that owes little to ideology or reason. A continuity of politics became its expediency, its opportunism. Policies were adopted, from one administration to the next, and at all levels of government, for purposes of short run expediences. Step-by-step diplomacy in the Middle East, SALT and START, industry bailouts, the arms buildup, growing reliance on monetarism—all continued notwithstanding disavowals and new labels. American presidents were buying time. Their political fortunes and policies were shaped by events and procedures over which they had less control. If they had a vision of America's place on this fragile planet earth, we saw little of it.

Emotion, intuition, and ideology may be getting played out now. The margins of national security and economic stability have continued to shrink. The country continues to be dependent on the forbearance of the Ayatollah Khomeini or the force of U.S. arms in the Persian Gulf. Interest rates remain high; the trade deficit continues to expand. The strategic arms race continues to escalate. Inflation has abated, and progress has been made against some excesses of prior administrations. But there is, we all acknowledge, little ground for complacency. High expectations of the future cannot be the product of any global tranquility—or inspiration and confidence in the government's purpose. Our expectations bounce around with the latest reports on the Middle East, the Caribbean, and the money supply. Even Mr. Reagan's military adventures abroad stir up little enthusiasm by historical standards. Their purposes are ambiguous at best.

Realists, ideologues, the nondescript are driven by the same political process. They react to similar pressures. It was under President Reagan, the economizer and free market ideologue, that the cost of farm programs rose to some $30 billion in one year, the federal deficit to $200 billion. President Carter imposed the "magic of the market" on airlines and truckers. The incongruities leave us with uncertainty. Stock markets react to weekly economic statistics, not from the unquestioning confidence in the future my generation knew when it was coming of age.

In its history, the nation suffered fools and thieves in politics, but prospered from the occasional wisdom of great men. A leveling process gradually curtailed the most egregious, and least mortal, sins of politics at some expense to the brilliance which occasionally enlivened it.

Given the choice, it always seemed safer, and certainly more popular, to protect against the abuses of politicians than permit the efficient and accountable service of public servants. Our founders recognized as much in their checks and balances and bicameral legislature. Civil service may have been the first great leveler of American politics. It protected mediocrity and diminished incentives to excellence in the bureaucracy. It became a popular obstacle to the popular efficiency and accountability promised by all candidates for public office.

Americans always had some difficulty balancing optimistic expectations of government with their skepticism toward government. In our time the skepticism tipped the scales against government in ways that left less prospect for sustained creativity and initiative. Jefferson had in mind an aristocracy of excellence. His reformed political party decreed that delegates to nominating conventions would be half

male, half female—never mind an historical prefer-
ence for excellence over egalitarianism or the public's right to decide, regardless of gender. Even
routine appropriation bills pass Congress with
difficulty—if at all now. Large parts of the government go from one Congress to the next, operating on
continuing resolutions; the appropriation bills of one
Congress are continued by the next. Necessary measures to increase the debt limit and authorize new
IMF quotas get hung up. The Congress was democ-
ratized; the power distributed throughout. We were
protecting ourselves from abuses of the congres-
sional seniority system and the political bosses. It
became more popular to oppose than to propose. It
was always easier. And the purposes for which government exists were less clear.

The challenges are more subtle than at times past.
They are not sharp like an attack at Pearl Harbor—or
a Black Friday in New York. Rarely did the country
ever respond before it was too late to avert suffering,
but always did it respond. Over time Toynbee's test
of challenge and response was met by the United
States. In a nuclear world, the oceans breached,
many of our natural economic advantages gone,
there are grounds for skepticism. The challenges are
real, however subtle. The response is uncertain.

The old pork barrels, smoke-filled rooms, and
paunchy political bosses largely disappeared. The
political machines did disappear. The reformers by
and large had their way. The political cartoonists fell
upon hard times. But the promised millenium did
not arrive.

A President died a violent death in Dallas, and a

myth was born against which no politician could measure up. Watergate followed Vietnam. And the nation suffered what the British historian, Macauley, called a "fit of righteousness." We moved again to protect ourselves from our own politics as if it was something alien and divorced from the people. The leveling continued. American historians who once hailed a strong President came to bewail an "imperial presidency." The country reacted, not to history, but its aberrations. It reacted in ways that had predictable, if unexpected, results. The reaction to the Bay of Tonkin Resolution was to institutionalize it—in a War Powers Act. Now the Congress sanctions the President's commitment of troops to Lebanon in order to uphold procedures intended to prevent such commitments. Introduction of the troops was itself caused by Congress's continuing subordination of national interests in the Middle East to political expediency.

President Nixon, the antipolitician, called politics a "game," as if the object were to win. And no one protested. A hundred years earlier, Lincoln, amidst terrible pressures, said, "I must keep some principle fixed within me, some consciousness of being somewhere near right." And, I suppose, no one remarked then upon the obvious. Politics is the means by which a people make the moral decisions which determine their welfare. We understood that better in Lincoln's day.

But television became the dominant medium. Its emphasis was visual and episodic. Mercenaries, known as campaign consultants, took over the management of political campaigns. The ever larger

financial requirements of campaigns came to dominate the thinking of candidates, their managers, and
the office holders. Political campaigns became, more
so than in the past, a business of money raising,
merchandising, and press manipulation. The national conventions became media events. Presidential candidates, forced to compete in fifty primaries
and caucuses, finally found themselves judged by
their jokes and applause lines in joint appearances,
known as "cattle shows."

The great Presidents of the last hundred years
were candidates of bosses—men, for all their faults,
with some interest in government, as well as in winning, some knowledge of the demands of public
office and the candidates. They and their precinct
captains were bypassed in our time by television.
The patronage system was wiped out by reform.
People migrated from the neighborhoods to the sub-
urbs, leaving black inner cities where once the mul-
tiracial machines thrived. The press took on power.
It could break a Senator Muskie, make a President
Carter. Now it is being exploited to build up a candidate with no chance of winning the Democratic
presidential nomination, nor any intention of run-
ning without it. Yet, Jesse Jackson is a threat to Walter Mondale, an authentic candidate. Race and gender became large objects of interest to the news
media. Senator Hart meanwhile demonstrates that
campaigns can no longer be energized by serious
ideas. The issues were trivialized. News became
another word for entertainment. The politicians had
less and less to do with politics.

It was in the nature of things for Americans with

their ambivalent confidence in politics to believe they could be protected from government by more laws. Government had been reformed before; but this time it was the failures of men, more than the systemic failures of the 1920s, which were at fault. And men, like social customs, were not to be easily reformed by more laws.

The methods of government became the ends of government. Politicians knew better, but they were made fearful and insecure by the failures of government, the breakdown of authority, and the passions that were loose. Skepticism was on the rise. The turnover in office was high. Party organization and discipline had broken down, leaving little security for politicians. They were cut loose to fend for themselves. They, myself included, dared not oppose anything labeled "reform" during that "fit of righteousness." We overreacted.

Common Cause cooperated with organized labor and organized business to reform the financing of campaigns. The interest groups, economic and ideological, were cut in. Citizens were largely cut out. The politicial action committees took over the financing of campaigns. The government was reorganized. It acquired an Energy Department, but little energy policy, an Education Department, but little education policy. It acquired sunset laws and more bureaucracy. It acquired sunshine laws and more opportunity for lobbyists. It enacted a Humphrey-Hawkins Law to end unemployment, and the country got more unemployment. It acquired an elaborate procedure to balance the budget and a budget unbalanced by $200 billion. It acquired

ethics laws which by implication sanctioned all behavior that was not explicitly prohibited. A slush
fund in earlier days was of doubtful propriety. Now it
is regulated.

Never, to borrow from Woodrow Wilson, was
nothing done so systematically as nothing was done
in the 1970s. Reform was an excuse for doing little.
Morality was not legislated. The missing moral
quality is courage—that always rare courage to be
right. But politicians lost courage with the growth of
public skepticism and the demise of institutions
which once gave them security and more freedom to
represent their conscience. Members of Congress
once repaired behind closed doors to represent the
public interest. When the doors were opened, the
interest groups entered. The scramble for conformity
with every creed and the demands of every powerful
institution gathered momentum.

Americans, subconsciously, were taking the easy
way out. It was easier for politicians and citizens
alike to look for self-adjusting mechanisms that could
make the right decisions with little discomfort for
anyone. For some it was an old innocence, an idea
that laws could cure all ills. For some it was a new
idea that associated excellence in government with
managerial skills. For others it was hyprocrisy. "Reform" was exploited for purposes of expediency. The
label, connoting virtue, was applied alike by politicians, civil organizations, and press to every manner
of overreaction. The expectations of government excited by this fit of righteousness were bound to be
disappointed. The efforts to instill more public
confidence in government by protecting the public

from government were followed by less confidence in government.

Government could be improved by competitive pay scales for public officials. But measures to make public service honorable and satisfying ran against the tide. It was more popular to pass ethics laws that discouraged public service. In Franklin Roosevelt's time, the volunteers in government known as "dollar a year men" were honored. Their ideas and talents from the private sector invigorated the public sector, and they had no ulterior purpose. Now "dollar a year men" are unlawful and volunteers do not flock to government because its purpose is less clear, less exalting.

The rapidity with which events move and the magnitude and complexity of issues in a pluralistic, nuclear world overwhelm institutions of self-government everywhere, perhaps less so the parliamentary systems of other nations. They tend to produce more experienced political leadership. By coincidence perhaps, they have publicly controlled, nonprofit channels of communication which disseminate truth to the public. But it is a universal phenomenon, found in industry as well as government. In our time the entrepreneurs and politicians have often yielded places to the managers of vast industrial and political enterprises, the bureaucracies of business and government.

In Lincoln's time the typewriter had yet to be invented. Today knowledge and information explode beyond the capacity of men to utilize with computers. A concern for management is right, but it should not be made a substitute for hard choices and new ideas. Managers and technocrats are no substitute for statesmen. They do not discover the new world, win the west, or put man upon the moon. Management is not an end in itself. The great Presidents may have been the worst managers. The great Presidents were practical men with some feeling for history, a vision, and an intuitive grasp of power. They appealed to our best instincts. They recognized that government was our means of collective action. They made its purpose justice and progress. They never exalted the nation to high levels of endeavor with balanced budgets, reorganization plans, or MX missiles. Wilson said, "We can afford to exercise the self-restraint of a really great nation which realizes its own strength and scorns to misuse it." James Madison would not have fared well with PACs and cattle shows, the evening news, a myriad of primaries and caucuses—the ingredients of our antipolitics.

Posterity, always neglected by politics in favor of things immediate, is impoverished, except by visions of a better world. Those visions have had a difficult time competing in this transistorized environment, as they did not two hundred years ago.

All in all, human qualities and informal methods which enlarged the nation's potentials for greatness, as well as for the corruption of its government, were drained from our politics. Efforts to make politics antiseptic went a long way toward sterilizing it. Now a generation has grown up in America knowing little of confidence in government, less of inspiration. The winning becomes as admirable as the governing for some who have known little else.

It is not possible to go back to a day that never existed, except in our nostalgia, or back to the days of boss rule. But a new honesty with ourselves would settle the pendulum somewhere near the center, between informal methods which for all their abuses served the nation well and this mechanistic politics which proceeds from distrust. Boss rule is not the answer, but the national conventions could be places for some deliberation by delegates with freedom to do more than ratify the results of early, out of the way primaries and caucuses dominated by party activists. The political action committees could be done away with, individual campaign contributors reenfranchised, limits placed on the amount spent by candidates. The salaries of public officials should require less personal sacrifice, the ethics laws be modified to permit more exchange of people and ideas between the private and public sectors.

When all the reforms are done, or undone, the great moral questions about our politics will remain. Who will have the courage to be right? Jefferson, one hundred and seventy two years ago, said, "Politics, like religion, holds up the torches of martyrdom to the reformers of error." All we will have done is restore some balance to the process and knock down some barriers to its impartiality, without restoring the machines which once gave politicians protection from the whims of opinion and the pressures of the powerful. Technology will multiply the channels of communication to permit more public access to truth. But in the end it is up to the people, their values, and their opinions—above all, their opinion of themselves.

What is the answer? The answer is Thomas Jefferson's. Trust the people. Trust them with the truth.

Men and women are ready to pick up the torches of political martyrdom. They are ready to lead. The American people are ready to sacrifice in causes they believe to be just and sound. They have been much put upon, but they would respond all the more energetically to some vision, some inspiration, some whispering of wings, however faint, above this apolitical cacophony of slogans, endorsements, polls, fund-raising appeals, and T.V. commercials.

The founders trusted the people to make wise judgments, given the truth. And they were right. People came for miles, on foot and by the thousands, to listen for hours to Lincoln and Douglas debate. They wrote letters of correspondence and marched in torchlight parades. They were a part of their politics. Now they have more responsibility. The franchise was made universal. The bosses were cut out. But they have less chance to exercise that responsibility. Debates are media events. The people are treated to polls of their opinion, with little chance to form it. They are removed from those who represent them in government. Familiar with their congressmen, they rate them highly and rank the Congress lowly. This is not the fault of the people, nor so much the fault of the politicians, as it is a wall which divides people and government. The people are removed from their government, the government from the people, and both from truth.

The process is drained of purpose, except for its own perpetuation. America's destiny must be renewed from generation to generation. Destiny requires our generation to build the world's institutions for peacekeeping, trade, money, and economic development. Destiny requires this generation, like all those which preceded it, to push ahead the frontiers of human experience and knowledge. We must explore outer space, use it routinely for mankind's benefit, or the Soviet Union will discover the new world. America's destiny means being different from the Soviet Union, ameliorating, not exploiting, the sufferings of people in the world.

Which way we go depends on those who control the people's right to truth. The most powerful, and least accountable, institution in our self-governing nation is the media. The other intermediaries are all but gone. The object of the media is profit—only incidentally truth and the nation's welfare.

The right to truth has become the most neglected of our civil rights, and the most difficult to enforce. Truth is elusive. It can be subjective. It is not readily identifiable. Representatives of the media claim the circuits are overloaded already. And, what is more, how can we judge? How can we assert our civil right to truth when we do not know what it is? We do not know what the media does not permit us to know. Least of all do we know of the glorious possibilities for an America at peace with itself—and its purpose.

With its material and human resources, and the values Americans cherish, converted by their politics to their policies, the country would have more grounds for confidence than in any time past. Never was it richer or more powerful in material things, nor its leadership more sought by the world. Never did science offer such potentials for human well-being.

Which way we go depends upon the people, not the politicians. The people are skeptical, but they know their country has the capacity to overcome the greatest challenges of their time. For Americans, challenges are opportunities. But if they want to avoid defeat, they must demand to know the truth.

DUE PROCESS OF LAW:
THE BULWARK OF A FREE SOCIETY

by

Andrew R. Cecil

Andrew R. Cecil

Dr. Cecil is Distinguished Scholar in Residence at The University of Texas at Dallas and Chancellor Emeritus and Trustee of The Southwestern Legal Foundation.

Associated with the Foundation since 1958, Dr. Cecil helped guide its development of five educational centers that offer nationally and internationally recognized programs in advanced continuing education.

In February 1979 the University established in his honor the Andrew R. Cecil Lectures on Moral Values in a Free Society, and invited Dr. Cecil to deliver the first series of lectures in November 1979. The first annual proceedings were published as Dr. Cecil's book The Third Way: Enlightened Capitalism and the Search for a New Social Order, *which received an enthusiastic response. He also lectured in each subsequent series. A new book,* The Foundations of a Free Society, *was published in 1983.*

Educated in Europe and well launched on a career as a professor and practitioner in the fields of law and economics, Dr. Cecil resumed his academic career after World War II in Lima, Peru, at the University of San Marcos. After 1949, he was associated with the Methodist church-affiliated colleges and universities in the United States until he joined the Foundation. He is author of twelve books on the subjects of law and economics and of more than seventy articles on these subjects and on the philosophy of religion published in periodicals and anthologies.

A member of the American Society of International Law of the American Branch of the International Law Association and of the American Judicature Society, Dr. Cecil has served on numerous commissions for the Methodist Church, and is a member of the Board of Trustees of the National Methodist Foundation for Christian Higher Education. Dr. Cecil also serves as Vice-Chairman of the Development Board of The University of Texas at Dallas. In 1981 he was named an Honorary Rotarian.

DUE PROCESS OF LAW:
THE BULWARK OF A FREE SOCIETY

by
Andrew R. Cecil

History of Due Process of Law

The right to due process of law rests on the Fifth
Amendment to the Constitution, ratified on December 15, 1791, and on the Fourteenth Amendment, ratified on July 23, 1868. The first is binding on
the federal government, the second binding on the
states. Both amendments command that no person
shall be deprived "of life, liberty, or property without due process of law." Although no concept is
raised more frequently in our judicio-legal process,
especially in appellate cases at the level of the
United States Supreme Court, the phrase "due process" has never achieved an exact definition. The
Constitution contains no description of those processes which it was intended to allow or forbid.
Neither does it declare what principles are to be
applied to ascertain whether any particular procedure is due process.

The concept of due process of law has historical
roots of ancient origin. Its existence does not depend
upon any statute or constitutional provisions. It had
been interwoven in the common law long before the
adoption of the Magna Charta. It was not alien to the
Justinian Code which survived the Roman empire

and which has given us one of the fundamental maxims of justice, *suum cuique tribuere* ("to render every man his due").

The history of the due process of law and of the law, broadly conceived, is the history of civilization and of mankind itself. Man has always recognized the need for a body of rules which could regulate his and his fellowman's actions—acknowledging, in that need, that he was at once prone to error in his relations to others and subject to some higher standard of judgment. Every civilization of which there is a record is governed by some sort of law, in the sense of a mandatory system enforced by power. Even before a written code of law, we find not anarchy but some system of rules.

It is necessary to distinguish betwen societies in which there is indeed law to protect men from one another (all societies have such provisions in one form or another) and those in which the individual has within the law itself standards of protection from society's abuse of its power over him. Most societies we call primitive have no such standards. These usually come only after—sometimes a long time after—the introduction of a written body of laws. We must also distinguish between "law," a generally understood body of rules that govern social behavior, and "laws," specific regulations promulgated by some central authority, whether a king or a legislature or a whole people voting together as in a Greek city-state. The desired end of law is justice, and it was often felt—for instance in Greece—that justice resided in the traditional law handed down from generation to generation and often not written down.

The great lawgivers, like Hammurabi and Moses, did not invent law, they merely articulated it. Hammurabi's Code, which is the earliest system of laws to have become generally known to most people, is in turn based on earlier legal systems in the Tigris-Euphrates valleys; these, no doubt, had their own predecessors. Moses, even after communing with God on the mountain of Horeb, did not bring back to mankind a revelation utterly new. The core of the Mosaic law is the natural law that God had already written on the hearts of men. There were new elements, to be sure, in the blazing insistence on loyalty and obedience to the monotheistic deity who had chosen the nation of Israel and in the special regulations that were designed to mark off that nation as a separate and consecrated people.

In Greece, the classic lawgiver in Athens, the equivalent of Hammurabi or Moses, was Solon. Little direct evidence remains of the substance of the legal code which he drew up. Scholars, however, have surmised that it represented a new standard of due process and equal protection of all. As far as the record goes, he was the first statesman on the European scene who proclaimed impartial protection for the noble and the commoner, the wealthy and the poor, the powerful and the powerless. In spite of the wide dimension of Solon's thoughts and projected program, the State remained omnipotent, and individual liberty, giving rights against the city and its gods, did not exist. The citizen had political rights to vote, to name magistrates, to have the privilege of being archon, but because of the sacred and religious character with which society was clothed, the

Greeks stressed the importance of the rights of the State.

To the southeast across the Mediterranean, even more than the thought of Greece, the Hebrew tradition was preeminently sacred and religious in character. But because of its devotion to the idea of the law as a written and unchangeable code—modified and elaborated upon first by oral tradition and then by written exegesis but always bound by the central revelation—Judaism contributed much to our sense of the protection afforded by due process of law.

We may take for an example the elaboration of the Judaic law on the matter of witnesses to testify. Although several brought witness against Jesus, their testimony did not hold up because of discrepancies. (Mark 14:57.) (It was only when the Priest questioned him: "Are you the Messiah, the Son of the Blessed One?" that Jesus replied, "I am," and went on to explain for what confirmation to look for.) In Jewish laws, a witness convicted of swearing falsely had to bear the penalty that would have been inflicted on the accused. (Deuteronomy 19:16-19.) The evidence of at least two witnesses was required for convicting an accused person (Numbers 35:30 and Deuteronomy 17:6 and 19:15.)

These basic requirements never changed, but they were refined in Rabbinic tradition. By the twelfth century, Maimonides could list ten classes of persons who were not competent to testify. Rules of inquiry, investigation, and interrogation evolved out of the biblical injunction, "Thou shalt then inquire and make search and ask diligently." Complex rules developed as to how to decide between conflicting groups of witnesses who contradicted each other in sworn testimony. Because of its profound respect for law as God-given and because of the unchangeable and unchallengeable basic rights and procedures laid down in the Torah, Judaic law afforded one of the earliest examples of procedural protection of human rights.

Under Roman law, the idea of citizenship implied the defense of individual rights against the unbridled power of the State. Roman citizenship meant liberty protected by law throughout a vast empire. At first restricted to patricians of Rome itself and later extended to certain plebeians, over the years the possibility of acquiring citizenship became a reality for many inhabitants of the Roman empire. When the Jews of Jerusalem seized the Apostle Paul and tied him up to be flogged, he asked the centurion who was standing there, " 'Can you legally flog a man who is a Roman citizen, and moreover has not been found guilty?' " The centurion "reported it to the commandant . . . and the commandant himself was alarmed when he realized that Paul was a Roman citizen and that he had put him in irons." (Acts 22:25-26, 29.) When the Roman governor Festus later asked Paul whether he was willing to be returned to Jerusalem for trial, Paul said, " 'I appeal to Caesar.' Then Festus, after conferring with his advisors, replied, 'You have appealed to Caesar: to Caesar you shall go.' " (Acts 25:11-12.).

Roman law served as a model for many centuries and still provides the basis for the legal systems of many nations of the world—largely because its provisions provided a bulwark of law and justice for its citizens. Except for its survival in some aspects of Canon Law, the Roman law was largely forgotten in Medieval times. The peoples who grew into the modern Western European nations evolved their legal systems out of tribal and later feudal law.

Many of the provisions of these systems seem incomprehensible to us. The concepts, for instance, of trial by battle or trial by ordeal (such as by fire or by water) are to us barbaric miscarriages or perversions of justice. In their own times, however, such provisions of the law might have even seemed enlightened or merciful. The courts were not places where due process of law or impartiality could be taken for granted; perjury was common and procedural remedies to prevent or disprove it were doubtful. Sometimes abandoning one's case to the proof of one's own might or to the providence of God was the last resort if justice indeed was to be done. The leading British historian of the law, Sir William Holdsworth, comments:

> "The age was superstitious, and miracles were plentiful because they were believed. It did not appear absurd to hope that God would protect the right. But it was also an age of corruption; and in a really corrupt age it is easier to meet a perjured claim by more detailed and particular perjury than to establish the truth. Battle, ordeal, and compurgation were suited to the age in which they flourished. Growing civilization demanded a clearer and more certain test." (Holdsworth, *A History of English Law*, Volume I, 7th Ed., Methuen & Company, 1956, pp. 311-312.)

In looking back over the history of the ages, it was the Magna Charta that provided a more orderly and deliberate method of protecting natural human rights.

Law of the Land

It is well settled that under modern law the phrases "due process of law" and "law of the land" are interchangeable and identical in import. The Magna Charta, called the "palladium of English liberty," in its thirty-ninth clause provides that no free man may be imprisoned, outlawed, exiled, condemned, or in any way destroyed, unless according to the law of the land. Concerning the expression "the law of the land," Lord Coke—one of the most eminent jurists in the history of England, whose doctrines of individual liberty had a profound effect on history—pointed out in his commentary on the Magna Charta that the Charter does not specify the "laws and customs of the King of England, lest it might be thought to bind the King only, nor the people of England, lest it might be thought to bind them only, but that law might to extend to all, it is said 'by the law of the land,' *i.e.* England." He continues:

"The law is the highest inheritance which the King hath, for by it the King and all of his subjects are ruled, and, if the law were not, there should be neither King nor inheritance. The Kings of England have always claimed a monarchy royal, not a monarchy signoral. Under the first, the subjects are freemen, and have a propriety in their goods and freehold in their lands, but under the latter they are villeins and slaves; and, my lord, this propriety was not introduced into our land as the result of princes' edicts, concessions, and charters, but was the old fundamental law, springing from the original frame and constitution of the realm."

In other words the rule that a person shall not be deprived of life, liberty, or property without an opportunity to be heard in defense is a fundamental right existing prior to the adoption of the Magna Charta. This rule is founded on the principle of natural justice and natural rights. Every person in the enjoyment of his natural rights has an inherent right to due process of law, which protects the citizen against all mere acts of power, whether flowing from the legislative or the executive branch of government.

Due process of law means, therefore, something more than the actual existing law of the land, for otherwise it would be no restraint upon legislative power. The question arises: To what principle are we to resort to ascertain whether any legislation or any governmental act is contrary to the prohibition of the Constitution as to due process of law? The Supreme Court of the United States has offered a twofold answer. First, we must examine the Constitution itself to see whether the act is in conflict with any of its provisions. If not found so, we must look "to these settled usages and modes of proceeding existing in the common and statute law of England before the emigration of our ancestors, and which are shown not to have been unsuited to their civil and political conditions by having been acted on by them after the settlement of this country." *(Den v. Hoboken Land and Improvement Co.*, 18 How. 372, 374 [1856].)

Does it mean that a process of law which is not otherwise forbidden can be regarded as due process of law only if it is sanctioned by the settled usage both in England and in this country? An affirmative answer would deny law the capability of progress or improvement. The cardinal principles of justice are immutable, but the methods by which justice is administered are subject to fluctuation. Each generation originates important reforms. Law draws its inspiration from new experiences, and the administration of justice changes with the progress of society and the advancement of legal science. The spirit of individual rights can be preserved by progressive growth of the law through adaptation to new circumstances and developments.

The Magna Charta gave the barons guarantees against the oppressions and usurpations of the King's prerogative, but did not limit the power of parliament, which was controlled by the barons. Because of the omnipotence of the parliament, arbitrary acts of legislation were not regarded as inconsistent with the law of the land. While in England the only protection against legislative tyranny was the power of free public opinion represented by the Commons, our Bill of Rights puts limitations upon the powers of the three branches of government, legislative as well as executive and judicial.

The maxims of justice and individual freedom of our law of the land perform a different function from the concessions of the Magna Charta that were wrung from the King. Our law of the land is designed to serve as a bulwark against all arbitrary acts of power and not only against executive despotism. The prohibitions of the Fifth and Fourteenth Amendments apply to all instrumentalities of the government, to its legislative, executive, and judicial authorities.

In the significant case of *Hurtado v. People of the State of California* (110 U.S. 516 [1884]), the Court held that due process of law in the Fifth Amendment refers to the law of the land, which derives its authority from the legislative powers conferred upon Congress by the Constitution of the United States, exercised within the limits therein prescribed, and interpreted according to the principles of the common law. In the Fourteenth Amendment, the due process of law refers to the law of the land in each state, which derives its authority from the reserved powers of the state, that include the fundamental principles of liberty and justice inherent in the very idea of free government and of the inalienable rights of a citizen in such a government.

Then the Court follows with this definition of due process of law.

"Any legal proceeding enforced by public authority, whether sanctioned by age and custom, or newly devised in the descretion of the legislative power in furtherance of the general public good, which regards and preserves these principles of liberty and justice, must be held to be due process of law."

Legal procedure may be changed from time to time, but always with due respect to the landmarks of liberty and justice established for the protection of the citizen. Due process of law is, however, more than legislative provisions merely providing forms and modes of attainment with no power over the substance of justice. Due process is founded on the essential nature of individual rights, which are not limited to life, liberty, or property. As Justice John Marshall Harlan pointed out:

"When the Fourteenth Amendment forbade any State from depriving any person of life, liberty, or property without due process of law, I had supposed that the intention of the people of the United States was to prevent the deprivation *of any legal right* in violation of the fundamental guarantees inhering in due process of law. [Emphasis added.]" (*Taylor v. Beckham*, 178 U.S. 548, 599, 20 S. Ct. 890, 1014 [1899].)

The meaning of the Fourteenth Amendment was highly debatable. Some, like Jusice Black, believed it incorporated all the guarantees embodied in the Bill of Rights. Others, and among them Justices Frankfurter and Harlan, advocated the concept that this Amendment incorporated fundamental values which may or may not be included in the Bill of Rights. The recent decisions of the United States Supreme Court call for the enforcement of the fundamental constitutional rights against the state's encroachment by the same standards that are applied against federal encroachment. Thus, for instance, the privilege against self incrimination of the Fifth

Amendment is applicable under the Fourteenth Amendment; the Fourth Amendment's standards concerning unlawful search and the Sixth Amendment's provision of right to counsel are fully applicable to the states. Identical prohibitions against the estabishment of religion or against abridging freedom of speech and the free exercise of religion are applicable to both the federal and state governments.

The guarantee of due process of law is absolute and not merely relative. It asserts a fundamental principle of justice rather than a specific rule of law, and thus is not susceptible of more than a general statement. Because the influence of constantly changing economic, political, and social forces is a vital factor in the interpretation of due process of law, its meaning has never been fixed and invariable in content. As a historic and generative principle, due process of law precludes definition. It is not surprising that in the Supreme Court some members have denounced decisions of the majority of their fellow Justices, particularly in regard to procedural due process, as "dangerous experimentations" offering "a balance in favor of the accused." A test offered by Justice Frankfurter based on a case-by-case approach—"Does this conduct shock the conscience?"—met with heavy criticism. Justice Black described Frankfurter's opinion as "merely high-sounding rhetoric void of any substantive guidance as to how a judge should apply the Due Process Clause." (A *Constitutional Faith*, Alfred A. Knopf, 1968, pp. 29-30.)

There is a general consent that due process of law should not be regarded as the equivalent of customary legal procedure since it is not limited to checking on departures from procedural regularity. It should also be conceded that it has never achieved, even in the field of "personal rights," a precise meaning. Because of the towering disagreements as to its meaning, the importance of the concept of due process of law can be realized only by weighing it against concepts of a legal system that disregards the basic standards of due process of law.

Legal System Without Due Process of Law

Marx believed that the legal system has a historical dimension and that, in accordance with the principles of historical materialism, the contents of laws and of legal institutions conform with the material interest of the ruling class. Thus economic relations determine the subject matter comprised in each juridical act. The Bolshevik revolution, therefore, sought to abolish the existence of law by destroying the old courts created by the czarist regime and by creating people's courts not bound by the law and conceived by the overthrown government. The judges were to be guided by their "revolutionary consciousness"; law was stigmatized as a tool of bourgeois exploitation.

In its first phase, communism, according to Marx and Lenin, cannot be fully developed economically and "entirely free from traces of capitalism." Marx admitted the inevitability of defects during the transformation of society from a capitalist basis to a socialist one. In the first phase of communist society, when it "has just emerged after prolonged birth pangs from capitalist society," the capitalists' standard of "right" will not disappear at once. With an equal performance of labor, one may receive more than others and one will be richer than another. These defects, states Marx, will disappear in the higher phase of communist society when the "narrow horizons of bourgeois right" will be transcended entirely and society will inscribe on its banners: "From each according to his ability, to each according to his needs."

Lenin defined dictatorship as "a power basing itself on coercion and not connected with any kind of laws." He goes further than Marx, however, when he argues that under communism there "remains for a time not only bourgeois right but even the bourgeois state—without the bourgeoisie." Since "law is nothing without an apparatus capable of enforcing it," he sees the need for a State which, while safeguarding the public ownership of the means of production, "would safeguard equality in labor and equality in the distribution of products."

Stalin and his followers went still a step further than Lenin by arguing that dictatorship of the proletariat, which is crucial in the period of revolutionary transformation, creates a State of a new type that in turn creates a new type of law—the Soviet democratic law. Proletarian dictatorship calls for the omnipotence of State power and for a law that will safeguard the new revolutionary mechanism of State authority and protect the interest of the toilers. Stalin rejected the concept of the gradual withering away of the State and the law. The stability of the laws, he declared, "is necessary for us now more than ever."

Stalin's constitution of 1936 implies the reinforcement rather than the withering away of the law.

Evgeny B. Pashukanis, one of the leading authorities in Soviet legal science after the Bolshevik revolution, rejected the idea of "proletarian law." Law, he maintained, is peculiar to bourgeois society and has its origin in commodity exchange. Since socialism will bring about the abolition of commodity exchange, the law will disappear together with the State. Devoted to his commodity exchange theory of law, which he identified with the Marxist theory of law, he predicted that private law will wither away when the institutions of private property and of market conditions have been eliminated. He thought that socialism should not impart a new content to the law, and found no reason to replace the bourgeois law with a new proletarian one. In 1937 he was liquidated by Stalin as a "legal nihilist" and as a member of the "Trotsky-Bukharin fascist agents." This fate was shared by others who adhered to the Marxist dogma of the abolishment of law.

The Stalinists rejected the "bourgeois" concept of due process of law. The purpose of their new law was to "smash the bourgeois state machine" and to inflict "a death blow on bourgeois law." There is no place for due process of law when the fundamental principles of liberty and justice which lie at the base of all our civil and political institutions are denied. The concept of due process of law as the observance of individual rights and protection against the arbitrary exercise of government power is diametrically opposed to the idea of the dictatorship of the proletariat. Stalin defined such a dictatorship at the

XVIth Party Congress as "the highest development
of state authority." It "represents the most potent
and mighty authority of all State authorities that have
existed down to this time."

Under such a dictatorship, the court is an instrument of the party and the judicial process is subordinated to the political end of assuring revolutionary
order and the authority of the State. Such law expressed the fundamental principle of State dictatorship, and the judicial process is used to legalize the
terror applied by the State and its secret police. It is
in the interest of the party and the ruling authority of
the State to sanction political terror within the context of formal legalism; the main function of the judicial process is to protect the dictatorship from any
kind of interference. The court is thus merely an
instrument of the party in power.

Stalinist Order

What were the results of this kind of administration of justice? Stalin used it as one of the chief
weapons in establishing the revolutionary order by
the elimination and destruction of anybody who
might hamper the building of the "socialist order."
The word "might" should be emphasized, because
under this system of contempt for due process of law
a person could be charged with a hypothetical of-
fense against the socialist order.

In the time of the great purges, the concentration
camps were filled with prisoners arrested on grounds
of being "potential spies" simply because they had
been outside the country. It was unimportant they
were sent abroad on a government mission; the im-

portant part was that, having spent a period of time in a foreign country, after their return they "might" have been "potential spies." Similarly, the concentration camps were filled with prisoners charged with being "socially dangerous." Stalin's "legal order" was first of all concerned with the relationship of class domination. The protection of the interest of the dominant class of toilers permitted the oppression of all elements which "potentially" could be opposed to the socialist system.

Under this system of punishing "potential" wrongdoers, not only violators of the new order were punished, but also the "indifferent" and the "passive," those who did not manifest affection for the new "morality," the new customs, the new ideas, the new Stalinist order. Such persons were regarded as dangerous to society; in concentration camps, the omnipotent State tried to "refashion" their intellects and consciences by destroying their old "prejudices," habits, and attitudes which did not benefit the ruling party's concept of the State order.

The axiom of the infallibility of the communist program is accompanied by the responsibility of "somebody" for its failures. In the 1932-1933 years of severe famine, the mass arrest of farmers took place as punishment for their failing to achieve the results of the economic plans approved by the party. The scarcity of food was explained by their "reactionary activity to undermine the security of the Soviet Union." The arrests were followed by confessions of sabotage. Tortures were inflicted to coerce the prisoners to confess to crimes they had never committed.

The mass arrests were chiefly organized in order to attain either or both of two goals: first, to convince the people that the communist party was perfect and that all economic failures were only a result of "subversive activity of the enemies of the Soviet people"; second, to supply forced labor on a massive scale.

Most of the major public works, including highways, railroads, canals, and tunnels, were built on the bones of millions of prisoners. In 1937 millions of innocent victims of Stalin's great purge were arrested and died in the camps. To supply labor, for instance, for the Moscow-Volga Canal, some of the victims were arrested under the charge of being a "socially dangerous element," proved by the fact that they had already been convicted once in the past. They were jailed to furnish unpaid labor under subhuman conditions, with no need to provide the minimum of goods which free workers expect.

Millions of people were transported to enforced labor camps from European areas occupied during the war by the Soviet Army, as well as from the Soviet areas liberated from the German occupation. Whoever survived the German occupation was a potential collaborator with the emeny. The population of the "liberated" republics was transported in "echelons" (cattle trains especially adjusted for mass exile) to the far north. They were simply sent there to furnish unpaid labor.

The family members of "politically dangerous" citizens were also subject to reprisals. The recently published *The Correspondence of Boris Pasternak and Olga Freidenberg 1910-1954* (Elliot Mossman, Ed., Harcourt Brace Jovanovich, 1982) reveals that

Olga Ivinskaya, with whom Pasternak had fallen in love, served two terms in a concentration camp because of her association with Pasternak. Pasternak's cousin Sasha died in the camps, and Sasha's wife Musya was also arrested. Pasternak's brother, Alexander, who for his work as designer and supervisor of the construction of the Moscow-Volga Canal received a medal from Soviet Chairman Mikhail Kalinin, rejected pleas that he petition the release from camps of some of his family members.

In the atrocity and horror of holocaust, Hitler runs a distant second to Stalin, who was responsible for the deaths of 20 to 50 million of his countrymen. Stalin was shrewder than Hitler was. Both of them inflicted upon millions of people brutal methods of extermination and of systematic moral and physical tortures. But Hitler murdered and persecuted to destroy nations and races; Stalin destroyed his "enemies" and "potential enemies" after exploiting to the utmost limit their ability to work. The concentration camp later or sooner became their tomb, but before their death, as long as they were healthy and strong, they had to give their strength to the State.

The Soviet Union won World War II. It annexed the Baltic countries and extended its control over Eastern European countries by establishing puppet governments, a method that had also been used by the Nazi invaders. But the Soviet Union shared with the Nazis a defeat in the battle for human minds. The war raised the Iron Curtain and revealed the communist theater of cruelty directed by a psychotic master who caused the deaths of millions of citizens. In the postwar period, numerous books and movies

described the Nazi concentration camps. The details
of Stalin's system of mass death now became available through the writings of Russian emigrés, to
mention only Solzhenitzyn's *The Gulag Archipelago*
and Antonow Ovseyenko's *The Time of Stalin: Por-
trait of Tyranny*. (The author is the son of one of the
heroes of the Bolshevik revolution whom Stalin had
killed.)

The horrors of the Nazi holocaust have received
ample attention from the producers of television
documentaries; not so the Soviet horrors. In May
1982, CBS broadcast a movie called "Coming Out of
the Ice," about a U.S. citizen who spent ten years in
Siberian concentration camps. The movie, an almost
unprecedented event in the history of television,
told the story of Victor Herman, who in 1931 came
with his parents to Russia to work in Ford's au-
tomobile plant in Gorky. As an exceptionally
talented athlete he set a world parachute-jumping
record. When toward the end of the decade the contract with Ford lapsed, Herman wanted to return to
the United States. The Russians refused to let him
out, since he refused to sign a document attesting
that his athletic record was set by him as a Soviet
citizen. He spent ten years as a prisoner in a slave-
labor camp.

The broadcast based the details of the life in a
labor camp on first-hand observations of Russian
writers such as Solzhenitzyn, Ginsburg, and others,
who in their memoirs have given a poignant account
of life in the camps. The scenes—of Herman beaten
up by the Russian interrogators for his refusal to
acknowledge Soviet citizenship; of him receiving

from his friend, who is being sent farther north, a trap that will give him a chance to survive by eating the rats it catches; of a dead man in a latrine covered with rats; and of a boxcar from which the guards pushed female prisoners to be raped by the male prisoners deserving "entertainment"—explained the true nature of a system that consumes its own citizens.

These scenes give a better understanding than any legal definitions of the significance of our constitutional individual rights and the importance of the guarantees provided by the due process of law clause. These scenes based on the testimony of an eyewitness about the life in Soviet concentration camps remind us of the answer given by the American historian, Charles Beard, who when asked if he could summarize the lessons that history teaches, said, "Whom the gods would destroy they first make mad with power" and "When it is dark enough you can see the stars."

In the post-Stalinist era the basic mood of the Soviet people, as described by the famous scientist and winner of the Nobel Prize for 1975, Andrei Sakharov, "is the passivity and indifference of the people induced to drink, burdened and tired by constant economic difficulties." (Sakharov has fallen into official disfavor, was exiled to the city of Gorky in the Russian interior and placed under surveillance.) Forced labor remains an integral part of the Soviet economic system. Although we do not hear about waves of political arrests of the magnitude that swept millions of innocent people under the Stalin regime, and the concentration camps may no longer serve principally to carry out the regime's political repression, the fact remains that the inmates of the labor camps continue to comprise a significant part of the labor force in a country where manpower is in short supply.

Shortages in manpower are solved by increasing the number of people in confinement. Business relations with the Soviet Union may, therefore, mean participation in their repressive system. It is not surprising that voices have been raised saying that in the building the West Siberian gas pipeline the Soviet Union will use the hundreds of thousands of convicted persons who are swept every year into the labor-camp system.

With Due Process of Law

Since the only hope of the people living in the darkness of totalitarian terror is for "the stars to appear," the writers of the Constitution tried to safeguard this country from the darkness of oppression and slavery by providing constitutional guarantees of the rule of due process of law. Although of ancient origin and founded on the principle of natural justice, this rule was enshrined in the Constitution to strengthen the protection of our inherent rights, indispensable to the existence of a free society. This rule, essential to the very concept of justice and ingrained in our national traditions, binds the federal and state governments in every one of its branches, departments, agencies, and other political subdivisions.

The application of this legal, or more accurately, philosophical concept as to the extent to which the State is permitted to exercise its sovereign power, in the last analysis, is a process of judgment by the court. When the controversy is argued before the Supreme Court, the philosophical views of the majority of Justices will decide the presence or absence of due process of law. The impact of the philosophical view of a majority of the Justices is highlighted by a shift of emphasis when personal liberties rather than property rights are involved. That shift has been described by the Court as follows:

> "Thus we find that while in recent years as the Supreme Court has increasingly recognized the right of a state in the exercise of its sovereign power incidentally to deprive individuals of their property, there has at the same time been definitely greater emphasis placed by the court upon the importance of the personal liberties secured to the individual by the Constitution and increased recognition of the place of the due process clause in protecting these liberties from impairment by the state." (*Douglas et al. v. City of Jeannette*, 130 F.2d 652, 658 [1942].)

What the shift of the emphasis means is that the changing interpretation of the Fourteenth Amendment, when applied to the State's exercise of its power inherent in sovereignty (such as police power, taxing power, or eminent domain power), is not intended to hamper the State in effective dealing with growing governmental problems. This shift does not mean, however, that the changing interpretation leaves the State the free play that would permit it to take arbitrary or unjustified action that would deprive individuals of the personal rights secured by the Constitution.

The impact of the philosophical views of the Justices of the Supreme Court, reflected in the changing interpreation of the due process clause, is highlighted by the 5-to-4 decisions in a long list of cases involving the application of the clause to the facts of a particular case. For an illustration, a case involving the religious sect known as Jehovah's Witnesses may serve. The members of this sect sold books and pamphlets without paying the fixed sum required by the city ordinances from all persons following certain specified businesses, trades, or vocations. The members of the sect argued that the ordinance as applied to them was unconstitutional, since it deprived them of their freedom of speech, press, and religion without due process of law. Five Justices construed the ordinance as a proper regulatory measure within the state's police power, to which liberties of the individual should yield. Four Justices interpreted the ordinance as a tax measure, which became—in violation of the due process clause of the Fourteenth Amendment—an instrument to suppress or even destroy the free exercise of speech, press, and religion when applied to the dissemination of educational and religious ideas. (*Jones v. City of Opelika*, 62 S. Ct. 1231, 86 L. Ed. [1943].)

Broadly speaking, the due process clause embodies a standard of fair dealing that satisfies a sense of fairness in every case of the exercise of governmental power. It is not imprisoned within the limits of any formula with a fixed content unrelated to varying circumstances. It is not a technical conception but a process of continued adjustment involving the exercise of judgment based on the experience of the past, sound reason, and the unfailing belief in the strength of democracy and in the sacredness of human rights. This stout belief requires observance of the general rules established in our system of jurisprudence for the security of private rights in any proceedings which may affect these rights.

In observance of these general rules, the Supreme Court has repeatedly stressed that the range of interests protected by procedural due process is not infinite and rejected the notion that "any grievous loss visited upon a person by the State is sufficient to invoke the procedural protections of the Due Process Clause." (*Meachum v. Fano,* 427 U.S. 215, 224, 96 S. Ct. 2532, 2338 [1976].) The application of the clause requires the following analysis: first, to determine whether a decision of the state implicates an individual interest encompassed within the Fourteenth Amendment's protection, always keeping in mind the nature of the interest at stake; second, if the protected interest is implicated, to decide what procedures constitute "due process of law."

For many years after the inclusion of the due process clause in the Fourteenth Amendment it was thought that the due process clause applied only to procedural rights. Gradually, the scope of the clause was broadened, and substantive rights were recognized to be embraced within its protection. The due process of law concept is, therefore, no longer restricted to purely procedural questions but is also involved in political, economic, and social issues that became a matter of judgment in our courts.

Procedural Due Process of Law

Procedural due process—which is the subject of far more litigation than the substantive kind—guarantees every person his day in court, an opportunity to be heard and to defend himself in orderly proceedings adapted to the nature of his case and in accordance with the generally established rules of our system of jurisprudence. To give such proceedings validity, they must be in a court competent by the law of its creation to pass on the subject matter of the case. The right of the person to be present before the tribunal which pronounces judgment upon questions of his life, liberty, or property in their most comprehensive sense must be safeguarded.

A host of practices embraced by a general standard of fairness falls into the category of guaranteed rights and privileges of the individual. Among these are the right to be informed about the nature and the cause of the accusation against him, the right to meet witnesses face to face, the right to counsel in criminal cases, the right to speedy and public trial, protection against self-incrimination, protection against cruel and unusual punishment, protection against double jeopardy, and freedom from unreasonable searches and seizures. These are only some of the examples of our civil rights and liberties that are protected by general standards of fairness and decency. They are firmly implanted in our society and constitute the irreducible minimum of due process of law.

The observance of procedural safeguards, wrote Justice Frankfurter, has largely been the history of liberty. To avoid high-sounding rhetoric, we shall illustrate the application of the concept of due process of law in testing the legality of governmental action by selecting three cases from among the mass of those brought before the Supreme Court of the United States on grounds of alleged denial or abridgement of procedural due process of law.

The first case deals with evidence obtained illegally by forcible extraction of the petitioner's stomach contents. In *Rochin v. California* (342 U.S. 165 [1951]), three officers of the State of California entered the home of a man under suspicion of selling narcotics. When he was asked about two capsules lying on a bedside table, the man swallowed them. After the officers' attempt to remove the capsules forcibly from the man's mouth failed, he was taken to a hospital where an emetic was forced into his stomach against his will. The two capsules were recovered and found to contain morphine, and on this evidence the man was convicted.

The Supreme Court overturned the conviction on the grounds that it was obtained by methods violating the due process clause of the Fourteenth Amendment. The opinion of the court was delivered by Justice Frankfurter, and his primary rationale was that "this is conduct that shocks the conscience." He compared the methods of the policemen to the rack and the screw, and reminded states that there is a general requirement that "their prosecutions respect certain decencies of civilized conduct." To sanction the conduct of the officers "would be to afford brutality the cloak of the law. Nothing would be more calculated to discredit law and thereby to brutalize the temper of a society."

The other case illustrates the sanction of the due process clause against the use of a confession wrongfully obtained—whether under duress by physical force or mental coercion or through illegal means. In *Beecher v. Alabama* (389 U.S. 35, 88 S. Ct. 189, 19 L. Ed. 2d 35 [1967]), the Supreme Court heard a case in which a Negro convict in a state prison had escaped from a road gang. The next day a dead woman was found near the prison camp. The prisoner was captured, tried, and convicted on a charge of first degree murder and given the death penalty. The Court reversed the penalty on the grounds that a preliminary confession was obtained only at gunpoint and that the signed confession was obtained five days later while the man was hospitalized, in intense pain, and under the influence of painkilling drugs so that he was in a "kind of slumber." The conclusion was that the confession was not "free and voluntary" but obtained by the exertion of improper influence.

In the interpretation of the due process clause, we may quite frequently find the Justices of the Supreme Court on a collision course. The case of *Breithaupt v. Abram* (352 U.S. 436, 77 S. Ct. 408 [1957]) may serve as an example. Justice Clark, alluding to the "whole community sense of 'decency and fairness,' " admitted into evidence a blood sample, extracted at the request of law enforcement authorities from the defendant as he lay unconscious. For Justices Black and Douglas, the admittance of such evidence was a violation of the Fifth and Fourteenth Amendments, since the taking of the blood sample was an assault on an unconscious and helpless man.

These three cases serve, among numerous others, as illustrations of the guarantee of due process, which demands that a law shall not be arbitrary or capricious, that the means selected shall have a reasonable and substantial relation to the object sought to be obtained, and that a denial of this guarantee is a failure to observe the fundamental fairness essential to the very concept of justice.

Substantive Due Process

The courts are called upon to take judicial action far less often in the sphere of substantive due process than in the procedural sphere. Substantive due process, as distinguished from procedural rights, refers to the content or subject matter of law. It inhibits the power of the state from depriving a person of life, liberty, or property by an act having no reasonable relation to any proper governmental purpose, or which is so far beyond the necessity of the case as to be an arbitrary exercise of governmental power.

Due process of law inhibits, for instance, the legislative power of the state from taking one man's property and giving it to another person without value received or without any contractual basis. This inhibition is valid regardless of the "merit of glory or value or need of the person on the receiving end of the transaction." A statutory wage-payment-for-voting-time provision, which had the effect of requiring an employer in Kentucky to pay an employee for four hours during which the workers absent themselves on election days to cast their votes, was declared by the court to be unconstitutional. Voting, said the Court of Appeals of Kentucky, is a public enterprise. "But if its maintenance is required by the employer group rather than by the entire, broad general public, then that amounts to a requirement of private maintenance of a public enterprise." (*Illinois Central Railroad Company v. Commonwealth*, 204 S.W.2d. 973, 975 [1947].) (This decision may not reflect the current general state of the law on wage payment for voting time.)

The Supreme Court took a different position in this debatable issue when in 1952, upholding a state law requiring employers to give time employees time off for voting, it stated: "Our recent decisions make plain that we do not sit as a superlegislature to weigh the wisdom of legislation, nor to decide whether the policy which it expresses offends the public welfare . . . [T]he state legislatures have constitutional authority to experiment with new techniques; they are entitled to their own standard of the public welfare." (*Day-Bright Lighting, Inc. v. Missouri*, 342 U.S. 421, 423 [1952].) Justice Douglas explained the attitude of the Court: "The judgement of the legislature that time for voting should cost the employee nothing may be a debatable one . . . But if our recent cases mean anything, they leave debatable issues as respect business, economic, and social affairs to legislative decisions."

The essential concept of substantive due process demands that the state's legislative power, which is broad and useful and extends to all public needs, should not, under the guise of promoting the public interest, arbitrarily interfere with private rights. The state's legislative authority may not unreasonably invade and violate those rights which are guaranteed under either federal or state constitutions by depriving any person of his property without due process of law.

Another illustration of substantive due process is sterilization legislation. An Act of Virginia of March 20, 1924, provided that the superintendents of certain health institutions might have sterilization performed upon any patient afflicted with hereditary forms of mental disease if such an operation were for the best interest of the patient and of society and if they complied with the provisions by which the law protects the patient from possible abuse. The constitutional issue raised before the Supreme Court was the alleged denial of substantive due process. The Act of Virginia provided full procedural due process of law but the appeal to the Supreme Court contended that sterilization "in no circumstances" could be justified under substantive due process of law because a sterilization order is on its face arbitrary, unreasonable, and capricious.

The Virginia statute was upheld by the Supreme Court. Since the public welfare, reasoned Justice Holmes, may call upon the society's best citizens for their lives it would be "strange if it could not call upon those who already sap the strength of the State for these lesser sacrifices often not felt to be such by those concerned, in order to prevent our being swamped with incompetence." Argued Justice Holmes: "It is better for all the world, if instead of waiting to execute degenerate offspring for crime, or to let them starve for their imbecility, society can prevent those who are manifestly unfit from continuing their kind." (*Buck v. Bell*, 274 U.S. 200, 207, 47 S. Ct. 584, 585 [1926].)

There are at least two reasons why the Supreme Court has abandoned substantive due process of law as "a perpetual censorship of state legislation." The first one, to which we previously referred, is the change of attitude toward a greater deference to legislatures as the originators of state policy and the guardians of the general welfare. This means that the Court gives more latitude to the state's police power, and exercises greater caution in labeling regulatory statutes as unreasonable, arbitrary, or capricious.

The doctrine of judicial restraint teaches judges to avoid unnecessary lawmaking. One point of view, as explained by Judge Learned Hand, stresses the duty to avoid unnecessary lawmaking in all constitutional cases regardless of whether the cases involve economic or personal freedom. Referring to the constitutional prohibitions, including the ones contained in the First Amendment, Judge Hand wrote: "Indeed, these fundamental canons are not jural concepts at all, in the ordinary sense; and in applications they turn out to be no more than admonitions of moderation." Consequently, the courts should not intervene "unless the action challenged infringes the Constitution beyond any fair dispute." (*The Spirit of Liberty: Papers and Addresses of Learned Hand,* Alfred A.Knopf Inc., 1960, p. 278.)

An opposing point of view rejects Judge Hand's interpretation as foreign to the First Amendment. According to Justice William O. Douglas, the due process clause of the Fourteenth Amendment requires only the legislature to act not without reason and not capriciously. The First Amendment goes much further since it was designed by its framers to

take from government the power to decide when
freedom of expression may "reasonably" be sup-
pressed. The idea that the prohibitions of the First
Amendment are not more than "admonitions of
moderation," wrote Justice Douglas, "has done more
to undermine liberty in this country than any other
single force." (*The Right of the People*, Doubleday &
Co., Inc., 1958, pp. 44-45.)

Although there may be no constitutional basis for
asserting a larger measure of judicial supervision
over "personal" than over economic values, the present position of the majority of Justices of the United
States Supreme Court is to give a much stiffer interpretation of the due process clause and a much
wider scope for judicial intervention when the subject matter is personal and not economic values.

The Supreme Court has edged closer and closer to
the position that the state is free to adopt whatever
economic policy may reasonably be deemed to promote public welfare and to enforce that policy
adopted to its purpose. The Constitution is not intended to embody a particular economic theory,
since it serves people with fundamentally differing
views. The judgment of the court should not, therefore, enforce its own abstract notions of the fairness
or unfairness of an economic policy. "The courts are
without authority either to declare such policy, or
when it is declared by the legislature, to override it."
(*Nebbia v. New York*, 291 U.S. 502, 537, 54 S. Ct. 505,
516 [1933].)

This position was aptly expressed by the Supreme
Court when it stated, "The day is gone when this
court uses the Due Process Clause of the Fourteenth

Amendment to strike down state laws regulatory of business and industrial conditions, because they are improvident, or out of harmony with a particular school of thought." *(Williamson v. Lee Optical Co., 348 U.S. 483, 488, 75 S. Ct. 461, 464 [1955].)* The Court is reluctant to assume the role of a third legislative chamber and prefers to limit its action to keeping the Congress and the state legislatures within their accredited authority. Still, where legislative judgment is oppressive and arbitrary, it will be overridden by the courts. The courts have the right to inquire whether a regulation infringing on individual rights is unreasonable or capricious.

In the area of individual or so-called "personal rights," when legislation collides with the Fourteenth Amendment and also with the First Amendment, the test of legislation is much more definite than the test when only the Fourteenth is involved. This is the second reason for the abandonment by the Supreme Court of substantive due process of law as a check on the infringement of individual rights that fall into the area of First Amendment freedoms. Much of the vagueness of the due process clause disappears when the specific prohibitions of the First Amendment become its standard.

Freedoms of speech, of press, of religion, and of assembly may not be infringed on such "slender ground" as the right of a state to regulate, for example, a public utility. In the latter case, the right to regulate may well include, so far as the due process test is concerned, power to impose all of the restrictions which a legislature may have a "rational basis" for adopting. However, in cases of freedoms falling into the area of the First Amendment, they are susceptible of restriction "only to prevent grave and immediate danger to interest which the state may lawfully protect." It is important to note, stated the Supreme Court, "that while it is the Fourteenth Amendment which bears directly upon the State it is the more specific limiting principles of the First Amendment that finally govern the case." (*West Virginia State Board of Education v. Barnette,* 319 U.S. 625 [1942].)

Equal Protection Clause

In addition to the due process clause, the Fourteenth Amendment contains an equal protection clause. The equal protection clauses of the Fourteenth Amendment and of the state constitutions constitute a guarantee that all persons subject to state legislation shall be treated alike, under similar circumstances and conditions, in privileges conferred and liabilities imposed. There is a tendency to merge the principle of equal treatment to all persons similarly situated with the concept of due process of law into a single guarantee. What is the reason for the vagueness of a distinction between equal protection and due process? The Fifth Amendment contains only a due process clause. Does it mean that the Congress in exercising its power of legislation may deny to persons equal protection of the laws?

To answer these questions we should review the history of the times when the Fourteenth Amendment was passed. Since the early years of the history of this country, the principle of equality has been accorded full recognition by the "law of the land," which was understood to be "a general and public law, operating equally on every individual in the community." Unequal legislation was invalidated by the courts on the ground that it violated the "inherent principles of right and justice," the "natural law," the principles of "natural justice," the "spirit of the Constitition," the decisions "of most respectable judicial tribunals," or the opinions of "learned commentators of the English law."

The incorporation of the Fifth Amendment into the Constitution reflected an already existing inhibition which restrained the powers of the government and asserted the duty of the courts to invalidate legislation inconsistent with consitutional guarantees. These guarantees included the equal protection of the laws. Although the Amendment does not contain the equal protection clause, it does not follow at all that the Congress in exercising its power of federal legislation may deny persons equal protection of the laws. All the guarantees of the Constitution are equal for the benefit and protection of all citizens of the United States.

The equal protection clause in the Fourteenth Amendment was primarily written for the liberated Blacks, although they are not mentioned in the Amendment. To remove the legal doubts about the validity of the Emancipation Proclamation (since it was made under the war power of the President) and to liberate slaves everywhere in the country, the Thirteenth Amendment was adopted. It provides that neither slavery or involuntary servitude shall exist within the United States, or any place subject to its jurisdiction. In practice the Thirteenth Amendment was found to be insufficient. The Supreme Court pointed out that in some states the former slaves continued to be forbidden to appear in towns in any other character than menial servants, that they did not have the right to purchase or own land, that they were not permitted to give testimony in the courts in any case where a white man was a party, and that they were subject to numerous discriminations.

The clause of equal protection of law in the Fourteenth Amendment was designed to prevent a state from making discriminations between its own citizens because of race, color, or "previous conditions of servitude." (See also the Fifteenth Amendment.) Chief Justice Taft made a distinction between due process and equal protection when he explained that "the spheres of the protection they offer are not coterminous." Due process tends to secure equality of law by offering a required minimum of protection for everyone's right of life, liberty, and property. But, writes Justice Taft, "the framers and adopters of this amendment were not content to depend on a mere minimum secured by the due process clause, or upon the spirit of equality which might not be insisted on by local public opinion. They therefore embodied that spirit in specific guaranty." (*Truax v. Corrigan*, 257 U.S. 312, 332, 42 S. Ct. 124, 129 [1921].) Due process, according to Chief Justice Taft, offers a minimum of protection, while equal protection offers a supplemental guarantee. As a supplemental guarantee, the equal protection clause has its own reason for existence and should not be regarded as an incidental right attached to the due process clause.

The Thirteenth Amendment and the two Amendments following were adopted more than sixty years after the first ten Amendments. Because of the experience of the Civil War, restrictions were imposed on the states which before the Civil War would have been impossible. Some of these restrictions were incorporated in the Fourteenth Amendment. In a very few years after the adoption of this Amendment, the docket of the Supreme Court became crowded with cases in which the Court was asked to hold that the state courts and state legislatures had deprived their own citizens of life, liberty, and property in violation of the due process clause of the Fourteenth Amendment.

It is not surprising that the courts were reluctant in the early history of the Fourteenth Amendment to give it a broad meaning. This reluctance was expressed by the Supreme Court when it pointed out that "there exists some strange misconception of the scope" of the due process clause as found in the Fourteenth Amendment and warned that the Fourteenth Amendment should not be viewed "as a means of bringing to the test of the decision of this court the abstract opinions of every unsuccessful litigant in a state court of the decision against him, and of the merits of the legislation on which such decisions must be founded." (*Davidson v. The Board of Administration of the City of New Orleans*, 96 U.S. 97 [1877].)

Because of changes in social values and concerns, the equal protection clause of the Fourteenth Amendment needed implementation to broaden the scope of protection against discrimination based on race, sex, age, creed, and physical handicap. Executive orders issued by our Presidents to curtail such discriminations lacked adequate means of enforcement. (The first such order was issued by President Franklin D. Roosevelt to create the Fair Employment Practices Commission.) The civil rights legislation of the last two decades—to mention only the Civil Rights act of 1964 and the Voting Rights Act of 1965, numerous federal regulations and state laws designed to eliminate discrimination, and the current array of legal measures to promote equal employment opportunity—offers more effective remedies than the equal protection clause of the Fourteenth Amendment against the barriers of discrimination.

Thomas Paine explained the principle of equality when he said: "The principle of equality of rights is quite simple. Every man can understand it, and it is by understanding his rights that he learns his duties; for where the rights of men are equal, every man must finally see the necessity of protecting the rights of others as the most effective security of his own." Advocating the Voting Rights Act at Howard University on June 4, 1965, President Lyndon B. Johnson called for equality not just "as right and theory but equality as a fact and equality as a result." Only the true intention of implementing this principle of equality and the effective enforcement of the guarantee of equal rights may crown with success the long and arduous struggle to put an end to the violations of the founding principle pronounced in the Declaration of Independence. "We hold these truths to be self-evident, that all men are created equal . . ."

Changing Trends

Because of due process and other constitutional guarantees, our homes are safe from unreasonable search on mere suspicion and we are safe from the moral and physical compulsion that wrung confessions from the rack and the screw. The makers of the Constitution undertook to secure conditions to protect Americans in their right to be let alone and in their right to the pursuit of happiness. These rights can be safeguarded only when society's public order is preserved. In accordance with the commands of our democracy and our constitutional principles, our society is also entitled to due process of law. As Justice Cardozo observed, justice "is due the accused, but it is also due the accuser."

Democracy imposes stringent norms restraining the overly zealous collection of evidence, but there is always the danger of shifting the balance in favor of the accused. Some of the decisons of the Supreme Court have become a focal point of attacks by Congress and law enforcement agencies. Dissenting Justices of the Supreme Court have voiced the sentiments of prosecuting authorities when they warned against hampering criminal law enforcement and rendering the task of these authorities "a great deal more difficult." Among the numerous decisions that have attracted heavy criticism for favoring the accused to the detriment of law-abiding citizens victimized by the rising crime in our country are the *Escobedo, Miranda,* and *Mapp* cases.

The Sixth Amendment guarantees the right to all persons prosecuted in federal courts to representation by counsel. In dealing with state cases, the Supreme Court considered the education and experience of the accused and the complexity of the charge to determine whether he had been harmed by the denial of counsel. In 1963 the Court repudiated this doctrine by extending the right of indigents to have counsel assigned in all criminal cases. The due process clause of the Fourteenth Amendment made the requirement of the Sixth Amendment of "the assistance of counsel" also obligatory upon the states. (*Gideon v. Wainwright,* 372 U.S. 335 [1963].)

This right to counsel was subsequently in 1964 extended to the preliminary hearing stage. In the famed *Escobedo* case, the Supreme Court reversed the conviction of Danny Escobedo, a young man with a record of numerous arrests who admitted his participation in a murder plot and was sentenced to a twenty-year term in prison, because he was denied the right to consult with a lawyer in the earlier stages of criminal proceedings. Justice Goldberg expressed the five-man Supreme Court majority position when he stated that, when the investigation is no longer a general inquiry into an unsolved crime but has begun a focus on a particular suspect, no statement elicited by police during the interrogation may be used against him at a criminal trial if "the suspect has requested and been denied an opportunity to consult with his lawyer, and the police have not effectively warned him of his absolute right to remain silent." One of the dissenting Justices, Justice Harlan, described this new rule as "most ill-conceived" and expressed concern that "it seriously and unjustifiably fetters perfectly legitimate methods of criminal law enforcement." *(Escobedo v. Illinois,* 378 U.S. 478, 493, 84 S. Ct. 1758, 1766 [1964].)

Two years later, in 1966, the *Escobedo* rule gained further extension to the interrogation stage following arrest. In the *Miranda* case, which has been bitterly criticized and viewed with alarm, the Supreme Court forbade the use of statements made by a person in custody unless he was told that he has the right to have an attorney with him before the interrogation starts. If the person in custody cannot afford an attorney, one must be provided for him free. *(Miranda v. Arizona,* 384 U.S. 436, 86 S. Ct. 1602 [1965].) The *Escobedo* and *Miranda* cases reflected the tide of social change that took place in the 1960s. The current of such change reversed its direction in the 1970s.

In 1971, for instance, Chief Justice Burger held that a statement inadmissible in the prosecution's case chiefly because of a lack of the procedural safeguards required by the *Miranda* case may, if its trustworthiness satisfies legal standards, be used for impeachment purposes to attack the credibility of a defendant's trial testimony. *(Viven Harris v. New York,* 401 U.S. 222, 91 S. Ct. 643 [1971].) In the *Harris* case, the defendant voluntarily took the stand in his own defense. Every defendant is privileged to testify in his own defense, but that privilege cannot be construed to include the right to commit perjury. In the *Harris* case, no warning of a right to appointed counsel was given before questions were put to the defendant when he was taken into custody. However, the shield provided by the *Miranda* decision, stated the Court, cannot be perverted into a license to use perjury by way of a defense, "free from the risk of confrontation with prior inconsistent utterances."

The defendant's credibility can be appropriately impeached by use of his earlier conflicting statement. The *Miranda* decision barred the prosecution from making its case with statements of an accused made while in custody prior to having or effectively waiving counsel. It does not follow, held the Court, that the defendant can turn the evidence inadmissible against him to his own advantage and provide himself with a shield against contradiction of his untruth. The dissenting Justices claimed that the *Harris* decision goes far toward "undoing much of the progress made in conforming police methods to the Constitution." They say a retreat from the *Miranda* case is jeopardizing the privilege against self-incrimination "if an exception against admission of tainted statements is made for those used for impeachment purposes."

As another example of changing trends, the jurisprudence in the application of the exclusionary rule which bars the use of evidence secured through an illegal search and seizure may serve. In 1913, the Supreme Court in *Weeks v. United States* (232 U.S. 383, 34 S. Ct. 341) held that in a federal prosecution the Fourth Amendment barred the use of evidence secured through illegal search and seizure. Since then the federal courts have operated under the exclusionary rule of *Weeks* for almost seventy years. In 1949, the question before the Supreme Court was whether the basic right to protection against arbitrary instrusion by the police demands the exclusion in state courts of logically relevant evidence ob-

tained by an unreasonable search and seizure because, in a federal prosecution for a federal crime, it
would be excluded.

The Supreme Court took the position that in the
Wolf case the rights guaranteed by the Bill of Rights,
comprising the first eight Amendments to the Federal Constitution, are not made applicable to the
administration of criminal justice in state courts by
the due process clause of the Fourteenth Amendment. Consequently, in a prosecution in a state court
for a state crime, the Fourteenth Amendment did not
forbid the admission of evidence obtained by unreasonable search and seizure though the evidence
would be inadmissible in a prosecution for violation
of federal law in a federal court because of a violation
of the Fourth Amendment. The Court stressed that
the security of one's privacy against arbitrary intru-
sion by the police is basic to a free society, but the
choice of the remedy against the violation of the
search and seizure clause is left to the public opinion
of a community, which can effectively be exerted
against any oppressive conduct of the police officers
responsible to the community they serve. (*Wolf v.
People of the State of Colorado,* 338 U.S. 25, 69 S. Ct.
1359 [1949].)

The immediate result of the *Wolf* decision was a
storm of constitutional controversy. There were
those who pointed out that a double standard exists
when evidence inadmissible in a federal court is
admissible in a state court. Since the very essence of
healthy federalism depends upon avoidance of
needless conflicts between state and federal courts,
the critics of the *Wolf* decision asked: Why may a

federal prosecutor make no use of evidence illegally
seized, but a state's attorney across the street may,
although he supposedly is operating under the en-
forceable prohibitions of the same Amendment?

Twelve years afer the *Wolf* case, in 1961, the Supreme Court overruled the *Wolf* decision. Justice
Clark, who delivered the opinion of the Court, held
that the rule excluding illegally seized evidence is of
constitutional origin, and, therefore, all evidence
obtained by unreasonable searches and seizure in
violation of the Fourth Amendment is constitutionally inadmissible in state courts. *(Dollree Mapp v.
Ohio,* 367 U.S. 647, 81 S. Ct. 1684 [1961].) "Nothing," wrote Justice Clark, "can destroy a government
more quietly than its failure to observe its own laws,
or worse, its disregard of the charter of its own existence." In his opinion, Justice Clark referred to the
warning of Justice Brandeis: "If the government becomes a lawbreaker, it breeds contempt for law; it
invites every man to become a law unto himself; it
invites anarchy."

Ten years after the *Mapp* decision, the Supreme
Court, in 1971, held that damages may be obtained
for any injuries suffered as a result of unreasonable
search and seizure by federal officials. *(Webster Bi-
vens v. Six Unknown Named Agents of Federal
Bureau of Narcotics,* 403 U.S. 388, 91 S. Ct. 1999
[1971].) This decision enforced further the rule
under which law enforcement authorities should be
deterred from using improper methods to obtain
evidence. The deterrence theory, or exclusionary
rule, wrote Chief Justice Burger in his dissenting
opinion, "has a certain appeal in spite of the high

price society pays for such a drastic remedy." Notwithstanding its plausibility, many judges and lawyers and some of the most distinguished legal scholars have never quite been able to escape the force of Cardozo's statement of the doctrine's anomalous result:

> "The criminal is to go free because the constable has blundered . . . A room is searched against the law, and the body of a murdered man is found . . . The privacy of the home has been infringed, but the murderer goes free!" (*People v. Defore*, 242 N.Y. 13, 21, 23-24, 150 N.E. 585, 587, 588 [1926].)

Justice Cardozo's warning is indeed forceful, but not less forceful is another consideration—the imperative of judicial integrity in the administration of justice and the imperative of constitutional restraints on which the liberties of the people rest. Among these liberties is the right to be secure against unreasonable invasions of privacy by law enforcement officers. The purpose of the exclusionary rule as pointed out by the Supreme Court in another decision "is to deter—to compel respect for the constitutional guaranty in the only effectively available way—by removing the incentive to disregard it." (*Elkins v. United States*, 364 U.S. 217, 80 S. Ct. 1444 [1960].) With this incentive removed, the administration of criminal justice by the federal courts that have operated under the exclusionary rule since 1914 has not been disrupted nor rendered ineffective.

The present U.S. exclusionary rule is not used in most common law countries. They have chosen to admit all evidence, however it is obtained, and to treat the punishment of police officers who have used illegal methods to obtain the evidence as a matter entirely separate from the issue of whether the accused has committed a crime. To protect innocent citizens from illegal search and seizure, offending police officers in some common law countries are punished through internal disciplinary procedures; in others, police officers are held criminally liable for misconduct, and civil damages are assessed against police departments. The punishment of police officers directly is intended to serve as a deterrence against illegal evidence gathering.

Gaining popularity is the idea that the present U.S. exclusionary rule should be modified to include a "good faith exception." Under this exception, a court would not bar the use of highly relevant evidence obtained during an illegal search made in the "reasonable good-faith belief" that it is constitutional. This change would correct the most grievous cases in which criminals get off because of some technical flaw in the conduct of law enforcement officers.

Ordered Liberty

The tide of social change reflects the standards of what, in a free society at a given time, is deemed reasonable and right. These standards do not become petrified as of any one time. In a free society, the courts are expected to enforce the rights that are basic to a free society. Of the fundamental rights, only some have the quality of eternal verity, while others cannot be confined within a permanent

catalogue of the essentials of fundamental rights and
are subject to the changing conditions developing in
a free society. As we discussed above, the present
tide has turned in the directions of increased deference to legislative judgment and of growing concern
with the upward trend in crime. The remedies offered by the due process clause may, therefore,
change from time to time, but always with due regard
to the landmarks established for the protection of the
citizen and of his security and property.

Decisions under the due process clause, as
explained by Justice Frankfurter, require close and
perceptive inquiry into fundamental principles of
our society. Our administration of justice is based
not upon transcendental revelation but upon the
conscience of society, ascertained as best may be by
a tribunal disciplined for the task and "environed by
the best safeguards for disinterestedness and de-
tachment." The faculties of due process may be
vague, but the mode of their ascertainment is not
"self-willed."

In each case, stated Justice Frankfurter, due process of law requires an evaluation based on a disin-
terested inquiry pursued in the spirit of science, on a
balanced order of facts exactly and fairly stated, on
the detached consideration of conflicting claims, on
a judgment not *ad hoc* and episodic but duly mind-
ful of reconciling the needs both of continuity and
of change in a progressive society. (*Rochin v.
California*, 342 U.S. 165, 172, 72 S. Ct. 205, 209
[1951].) As Justice Cardozo twice wrote for the
Court, due process of law is a summarized constitutional guarantee of respect for those personal im-

munities which are "so rooted in the tradition and conscience of our people as to be ranked as fundamental" *(Snyder v. Massachusetts,* 291 U.S. 97, 105, 54 S. Ct. 330, 332 [1933]) or are "implicit in the concept of ordered liberty." *(Palko v. Connecticut,* 302 U.S. 319, 325, 58 S. Ct. 149, 152 [1937].)

The very nature of due process negates any inflexible concept, since it varies with the subject matter and the necessities of the situation. The facts and circumstances of each case may vary, but the purpose of due process never varies—it defines the rights of the individual and delimits the powers which the state may exercise. Its fundamental requirement is to avoid unfairness to individuals resulting from unconstitutional evidence and remedies. In our independent courts was vested the responsibility to resist every encroachment upon the rights stipulated for in the Constitution by its declaration of rights.

In discharging this responsibility it cannot be overlooked that even fundamental rights are not absolute. Decades ago Justice Holmes, referring to the right of free speech, made the famous statement: "The most stringent protection of free speech would not protect a man in falsely shouting fire in a theatre and causing a panic." He referred to the society as "the one club to which we all belong." Above all rights rises our duty to the community and concern about its welfare. In application of the due process clause, the courts have to seek accommodations between individual rights and the people's "concept of ordered liberty." The court draws the line of accommodation by the empiric process of "inclusion and exclusion," by the gradual process that responds to sensible claims by citizens to their rights vital to the maintenance of a free democratic society.

DEMOCRACY, ECONOMICS, AND RADICAL PLURALISM

by

Richard John Neuhaus

Richard John Neuhaus

Born in Pembroke, Ontario, Canada, Pastor Neuhaus was educated in Ontario, Nebraska, and Texas. He studied theology at Concordia Theological Seminary, St. Louis, and philosophy and sociology at Washington University, St. Louis, and Wayne State University, Detroit. He served pastoral internships in Detroit and Chicago.

For seventeen years he was senior pastor of a low-income black and hispanic parish in Brooklyn, New York. He is now "Pastor on Assignment" for the East Coast Synod of the Association of Evangelical Lutheran Churches (AELC). Over the years he has played a leadership role in numerous organizations dealing with civil rights, peace, international justice, and religious ecumenism. His work and writing have been the subject of feature articles in Time, Newsweek, The New York Times Magazine, *and scholarly publications. In 1982 he received the "Faith and Freedom Award" from the Religious Heritage Foundation of America.*

For eight years he was Senior Editor of Worldview, *a monthly journal on ethics and social changes. He is currently editor of* Forum Letter, *a commentary on religion and culture, and Project Director at the Council on Religion and International Affairs, an Andrew Carnegie foundation in New York City. His current writing projects include a book on religion and politics in South Africa and another on secularization in American society.*

Among the books Pastor Neuhaus has written are In Defense of People *(1971), the first book-length critique of environmentalism as it relates to ideas of social justice;* Time Toward Home: The American Experiment as Revelation *(1975), a critically acclaimed study of the nature of American democracy;* Christian Faith and Public Policy *(1977), a detailed analysis of connections between Christian faith and public policy making; and* Freedom for Ministry *(1979), a critical affirmation of the theory and practice of Christian ministry.* The Naked Public Square, *concerning religion and democracy in America, will be published in 1984.*

DEMOCRACY, ECONOMICS, AND RADICAL PLURALISM

by Richard John Neuhaus

I take it that commitment to democracy means commitment to a pluralistic and open society. Democracy means more than that, but it also means no less than that. In this context, the terms "pluralistic" and "open" are almost synonymous. An open society is marked by the free interplay of different worlds, of different ways of viewing the world, of different individual and communal ways of being in the world. In short, an open society is pluralistic.

That ours is and should be a pluralistic society is a matter of reasonably settled public consensus. That consensus is of relatively recent vintage, however. Forty years ago, and for a hundred years before that, pluralism was frequently seen not as a virtue but as a problem. The problem was created by mass immigration to the United States of people of radically disparate cultures. Then it was thought that the great task was to "Americanize" the so-called immigrant hordes. The instrumentality for doing this was the so-called American melting pot. Domestically, the task was to include black Americans in the mainstream of the society. The instrumentality for doing this, up through the civil rights movement of the 1950s and early 1960s, was integration. Today both the melting pot and racial integration are widely perceived as destructive myths that have been most deservedly discarded. Pluralism, which was once seen as the problem is now hailed as the answer. What was once deplored as a vice is now celebrated as a virtue.

As indicated at the outset, most of us undoubtedly affirm pluralism. It is part of our understanding of democratic freedom. In addition, it is essential to the variety and vitality of life in America. Pluralism is at the heart of the robust and sometimes maddening diversity and contradiction which distinguish our society from those societies that are more "rationally" ordered. And yet today voices are raised—at all points on the political and social spectrum—which question whether perhaps pluralism has gone too far. The question is not always put in those terms but I believe that is the substance of the growing anxiety about the limits of pluralism.

Pluralism cannot be sustained in a cultural vacuum. Pluralism as a social value cannot be sustained in the absence of other social values. Pluralism is desirable and sustainable within a cultural matrix, within an enveloping world of shared moral discourse. Today that cultural matrix is in an advanced stage of dissolution. Where there is a cultural matrix, pluralism is tempered by other values and ideals— justice, compassion, moral purpose, and an understanding of rights which all are bound to respect. In the absence of such a cultural matrix, pluralism in isolation from other values is no longer tempered pluralism. It becomes total pluralism. Total or radical pluralism is no longer the pluralism of the lively interaction of diversities. It becomes a pluralism of meanings and moralities, a pluralism which makes significant interaction impossible. Total pluralism results in public speech that is not discourse but only confusion. Our encounters in public space are marked not by tolerance but by mutual incomprehension. In the situation of total pluralism, even genuine disagreement is precluded, for there are not shared points of reference by which either agreement or disagreement can be achieved.

As it was and still is popularly said, "Everybody should do his or her own thing." There is an undeniable winsomeness to the proposition. The proposition is closely connected to what has been meant by freedom in the American experiment. Yet the proposition that everybody should do his or her own thing is clearly a perilous foundation on which to base a cultural matrix, not to mention a public philosophy. Pluralism pushed to its totalist conclusion is individualism run amok. There are exquisite and little noticed ironies in this connection. First, total pluralism destroys the communities of cultural diversity which in American history gave rise to pluralism as a positive metaphor. Communities— ethnic, racial, linguistic—cannot survive unqualified individualism. Second, total pluralism destroys the shared moral meanings by which diversity, individual and communal, is protected. That is to say, pluralism must be morally justified in behavior, politics, and law. Some may believe that pluralism is its own reason for being, but that will not protect pluralism from those who do not share that belief. The value of pluralism must be justified from beyond itself, as it were. It is precisely the justification of pluralism, however, a justification which depends upon a larger world of shared moral discourse, that total pluralism assaults. A third irony follows from this: Total pluralism is the death of pluralism, either tempered or total. Again, by total pluralism I mean what some describe as moral pluralism—the denial of any intersubjective meanings that are morally binding. Total pluralism is the prelude to authoritarian or totalitarian imposition of meaning. As Dostoevsky's Grand Inquisitor knew, and as the totalitarians of our day have demonstrated with brutal effect, freedom in isolation from moral purpose or moral limits is intolerable and unsustainable.

In the situation of total pluralism, public life becomes, in the memorable words of Alasdair MacIntyre, "civil war carried on by other means." The civil war will be won by those forces best able to meet the majority's hunger for coherent meaning. The meaning offered need not be especially persuasive or even intelligible. If the situation is desperate enough, the promise of order instead of chaos will be coherent meaning enough.

In the situation of total pluralism, moral judgments are characteristically resented as a violation of freedom. Those who make such judgments, at least in public, are accused of "imposing their values upon others." The resentment is especially severe if such moral judgments are "tainted" by association with religious belief. This pattern of thinking might also be described as perverse pluralism, thus suggesting that pluralism itself is a value greatly to be cherished. It is a pattern that affects every aspect of our life together, including the way we think about the economic system associated with the American democratic experiment.

In current economic thought, radical pluralism finds its parallels in the thinking of some of the more outspoken advocates of a "free market" economy. One thinks, for example, of Milton Friedman. George Gilder also falls into this category, although he does make some intriguing but finally unpersuasive efforts to ground capitalism in a normative ethic. In its most strident form, the economic dimension of total pluralism is frequently articulated by those who call themselves libertarians. The more extreme in this group insist that every aspect of our life together can best be understood and handled by the metaphor and the mechanism of the free market. In this view, we all do our own things and the "invisible hand" will attend to the consequences—which will generally be benign, or at least less dreadful than under alternative forms of political economy. As has frequently been noted, the extreme libertarian view violates conventional understandings of what is left and what is right. It is so far right as to seem left, and so far left as to seem right.

I am not a professional economist, and my purpose, therefore, is not to analyze the economic merits of the several schools of thought now current. My purpose, rather, is to argue that, also in the sphere of the economic, democratic society cannot be sustained apart from a cultural matrix which provides moral meaning. More specifically, I propose to examine briefly the ways in which religion in America has tried to morally inform our thinking about economic behavior. In the course of our examination it will become evident that religion has been supportive of democratic capitalism and of varieties of socialism, but it cannot abide the total pluralism of the libertarian.

When one mentions religion and economics, the name that most immediately comes to mind is that of Max Weber. His influence was paramount in imprinting on our minds the connections between a particularly Calvinist form of Christianity and the rise of capitalism. In America his thesis received powerful support in the civil virtues once cultivated by what we today call mainline Protestantism. By mainline Protestantism I mean those older, culturally established, and thoroughly Americanized churches which inherited and embraced the Puritan mandate to give moral definition to the American social experiment. Up through the beginning of this century, the most influential Christian leadership generally celebrated, in the words of Andrew Carnegie, "the gospel of wealth." The linkage seemed to be secure between Protestant individualism and economic enterprise, between righteousness and prosperity. Justice in economic life included not only the obligation to share wealth but also the obligation to produce wealth.

Already by the last quarter of the nineteenth century, however, there was a significant counterforce, usually referred to as the social gospel movement. Dismayed by the perceived evils of the "robber barons" of American capitalism, overwhelmed by the dislocations which accompanied massive immigration, plus rapid industrialization and urbanization, the leaders of the social gospel movement began to urge that there was something fundamentally wrong with the economic system itself. To use the terms of today, they moved away from the "bandaid" approach of charity toward the analysis of the "systemic" evils of capitalism. As early as 1887, social gospel leader Washington Gladden was advancing the analysis of class warfare:

> "The state of the industrial world is a state of war. And if war is the word, then the efficient combination and organization must not all be on the side of capital . . . While the conflict is in progress, labor has the same right that capital has to prosecute the warfare in the most effective way. If war is the order of the day, we must grant to labor belligerent rights." (Quoted in Robert T. Handy, *A Christian America: Protestant Hopes and Historical Realities*, Oxford University Press, 1971, p. 159.)

Historian Robert Handy adds, "Though the self-conscious advocates of this new interpretation never became a majority party in any given denomination, in the years prior to World War I they were highly articulate in pulpit, platform, and press and evoked wide interest in social questions." (*A Christian America*, pp. 158-159.) Gladden, Walter Rauschenbusch, Richard Ely, and others represented a direction that came to dominate thinking about Christianity and social reform. Once again, Handy puts it well:

> "The notes of humanization, of sacrificial service, and of the servant role of the church were . . . accommodated to the familiar [Puritan] quest for a Christian civilization. The social gospel advocates were men of their time who operated

largely within the patterns of the quest for a Protestant America. The new social Christianity had a vision of vastly better human society, but it was essentially the old vision of a religious nation socialized." (A Christian America, p. 161.)

Their thinking was reflected in the social statements of the old Federal Council of Churches and today lives on its successor body, the National Council of Churches. Then and now it may not have reflected the thinking of most church members, but it was and is the dominant mindset within the religion-and-society bureaucracies of the several denominations. Both accuracy and fairness require us to remember, however, that preaching socialism in the 1880s—and maybe even in the 1930s—was very different from preaching socialism today. Then the condition of labor in industrializing societies was in fact often brutal. Then it was not yet apparent that capitalism could work to the great benefit of labor. Then the connection between socialism-in-practice and totalitarianism was not evident. The social gospel leaders lived before the manifest economic and human failures of sundry socialist experiments. They lived before the Gulag Archipelago. The Christian opponents of capitalism today are, of course, operating in a quite different context. The continuity in rhetoric with the social gospel movement is accompanied by profound discontinuities in historical experience. There remains, however, a clear continuity of intention, not only with the social gospel movement but with the Puritan tradition underlying it; the continuing intention is to provide a normative moral meaning for economic activity.

There are important differences among people who profess to favor socialism in one sense or another. These differences are overlooked by Americans who lump all socialisms together and make socialism equivalent to communism. Even some of our secular neoconservative thinkers today, such as Daniel Bell, still call themselves socialists. That may reflect only nostalgic loyalty to youthful enthusiasms when they were students in the thirties. And figures on the left insist that their devotion is to democratic socialism, although not all of them are as honest as Michael Harrington in admitting that the historical evidence from every socialist experiment to date offers little support for the hope that socialism can, in fact, be democratic. The socialism prevalent among people in the church-and-society curia of mainline denominations might be called "soft socialism." It is an afterglow of the social gospel movement and results in large part from that movement's appropriation of some of the best moral language.

Community, self-sacrifice, sharing, equality, solidarity with the poor and oppressed—such are the words that evoke a warm response from the sensitized conscience. And to be sensitized—to have one's consciousness raised—is in some sense to feel guilty, to be haunted by the suspicion that we have more *because* others have less. The resulting, and perfectly understandable, bias in economic thinking is toward redistribution and equality rather than toward production and opportunity. Soft socialists do not advocate violent revolution (at least not here or not yet), nor do they call for nationalizing the means of production (at least not totally). With reference to historically identifiable doctrines, it is hard to say in what ways they are socialists at all. But the language of socialism—the cultural matrix it invokes—is more in accord with their moral sensibilities. If they are unsure about whether or in what way they are socialist, of one thing they are certain: They are anticapitalist. Capitalism is seen as the antithesis to justice; it is a moral affront to those who describe themselves, somewhat immodestly, as the constituency of conscience.

Mixed with this soft socialism of vague collectivist sentiment is another variety of socialism. It sees itself as hard, determined, prepared to pay the necessary price for the creation of the "New Man in the New Society." Sometimes it says that it is not really Marxist but is merely employing "Marxist analysis." At other times it does not shrink from declaring its Marxist and even Marxist-Leninist allegiance. Its overarching rationale is usually presented in terms of "liberation theology." Here again, not all liberation theologies should be lumped together. In the version most pertinent to our present consideration, liberation theology is chiefly, but not exclusively, associated with Latin America. Some of its literature is very impressive. Men such as Gustavo Gutierez and Juan Luis Segundo have written its most detailed texts. In this country, some of the central themes are related to black liberation, women's liberation, gay liberation, and other movements aimed at overthrowing what are viewed as repressive social customs and policies. But in its most aggressive form, its purpose is not to ameliorate one social discontent or another but is to bring about a wholesale and radical restructuring of the social and economic order. The basic proposition is that the root cause of the world's injustices—such as imperialism, colonialism, neocolonialism, racism, sexism, and militarism—is capitalism. That is the major premise. The minor premise is that the United States and its multinational corporations are the chief carriers of the capitalistic disease. The conclusion is therefore inescapable: The church must get on the right side of the global struggle to cast off the burden of American oppression.

Liberation theology in its more absolutist form is in large part a Latin American and Roman Catholic phenomenon. It is also embraced and promulgated, however, from essentially Protestant centers such as the World Council of Churches (WCC). In the face of some undiscriminating criticism of the World Council, it should be emphasized that the World Council is a multifaceted institution. It receives and I believe it fully deserves the support of ecumenical Christians for its "Faith and Order" work toward a fuller expression of Christian unity in the world. But there are other aspects of the World Council which have not met with such widespread approval. From its Geneva headquarters the WCC issues militant statements of support and considerable financial aid for various liberationist struggles, notably in South Africa. Sometimes such support is phrased in terms of humanitarian aid. At other times, as in a recent World Council book, *Toward a Church of the Poor* (ed. by Julio Santa Ana, 1979), the commitment to global revolution is made explicit beyond doubt.

Within the member churches of the WCC, misgivings about this liberationist commitment are being voiced with greater frequency and effect. Also on the Roman Catholic side, Pope John Paul II in particular has attempted to check what he views as the excesses of liberation theology, while probing toward alternative strategies for a distinctively Christian way of working with and for the oppressed.

The agonized probings of Pope John Paul, however, are alien to the revolutionary confidence that marks much Christian sociopolitical thinking today. The North American popularizer of liberation theology, Robert McAfee Brown, articulates what is the assured consensus in some circles: "Liberation theology tells us that we are on the wrong side and that if we do not change sides things will be very rough for us in the future, but we immediately realize that if we change sides, things will be very rough for us in the present." (*Is Faith Obsolete?* Westminster Press, 1974, p. 124.) The World Council has established a Commission on the Church's Participation in Development (CCPD). According to studies produced by CCPD, Christianity has no redemptive purpose apart from "radical social and political change." Before the churches can liberate others, however, they must themselves be liberated. The CCPD puts it this way: "Without the salvation of churches from·their captivity in the interests of the dominating classes, races and nations, there can be no saving church." (*Separation Without Hope?: Essays on the Relation Between the Church and the Poor During the Industrial Revolution and the Western Colonial Expansion*, ed. by Julio de Santa Ana, World Council of Churches, 1978, p. 186.)

On this view, it is naive to think that Christians are called simply to love and serve the less fortunate. Love "remains incomplete unless it is accompanied by militant action to promote justice at the level of the social structures and in accordance with the realities and the requirements of concrete social struggles." *(Separation Without Hope?*, p. 183.) Those who strive to meet human needs and alleviate suffering are a distraction from the struggle unless their work is joined to revolutionary praxis. Without "militant action to promote justice," the amelioration of human misery can only make unjust situations more tolerable and thereby delay the day of revolutionary reckoning.

As it is not enough for the church to be serving the poor in meeting human needs, so it is not enough that the churches actually incorporate and be led by the poor. Just because a church is made up of poor people does not mean that it is a "church of the poor." CCPD explains: "The Pentecostal churches in certain parts of Latin America or Africa are described as 'churches of the poor,' but [as in the case of the Pentecostals in Chile] these groups, although made up of poor people, do not really represent a 'popular' mentality. Far from claiming their rights, they are actually seeking to climb the ladder in society, and for this purpose their assimilation of attitudes and values via their religious allegiance can be a useful tool." *(Separation Without Hope?*, p. 180.)

Here we have a remarkable proposition. It is said that the poor have a powerful claim upon our concern, but we are under no obligation to the poor who are trying to better their situation within existing economic and political structures. Their religious allegiance is only a "useful tool" for the advancement of their selfish purposes. Far from standing in solidarity with these poor, they are to be condemned as the enemies of the struggle for justice. There are the poor and then there are the poor. One is reminded of the old ideas of "the deserving poor," an idea that is supposedly discredited. But now the deserving poor are those who share our understanding of social, political, and economic change. We certify as deserving poor, and even as authentic brothers and sisters in Christ, those who are part of the struggle. The decision is ours. It is an odd position to be taken by Christians who ordinarily condemn ethnocentricism as well as cultural and political imperialism.

Those who espouse this view usually insist that the revolutionary change they have in mind is not part of the superpower games played by the United States and the Soviet Union. Their concern, they contend, is for indigenous revolution, for the poor who are struggling toward that change appropriate to their own social and cultural circumstances. Nonetheless, at other times the bias in favor of the Soviet Union is admitted. For example, a CCPD document offering a global overview puts it this way: "When we look at the basic causes of these confrontations [between the superpowers] we see that there has always existed—at least in one of the parties to the conflict—the desire for greater equity in society." (Good News for the Poor, p. 105.) The party in question, we may be sure, is not the United States.

Because the liberationist vision is religious in nature, its reach is expansive. CCPD quotes approvingly this understanding of our situation: "The apocalyptic crisis has descended upon our age, not prematurely as in the time of Jesus, but in the fullness of time. Opportunity as it confronts us is also the final sifting of chaff from wheat, the day of judgment. The Church may try, but it cannot succeed today in crucifying the Christ. The new Christ should be like an insurgent Proletariat, the uprisen people of God, and the Church which fails to do him reverence must be cast forth into the outer darkness. The Day of the Lord is at hand." (*Ibid.*, p. 108.) Here we see that not only does Christ bless the revolution, not only is he engaged in the revolutionary struggle, the struggle *is* Christ.

Is this an instance of religious extremism, even fanaticism? It would be difficult to deny it. It is not sufficient to condemn such fanaticism, however. To paraphrase Spinoza, transcendence abhors a vacuum. When in a situation of radical pluralism normative ethical judgment is excluded from public discourse, a vacuum is created which invites transcendent visions, no matter how bizarre. Those who wanted to exclude religious extremism from public discourse have ended up excluding religion and religiously grounded values. Again, the resulting naked public square is a transitional phenomenon. It cannot and does not remain naked. It will be clothed by an alternative vision of compelling drama and hope.

It is one of the great sadnesses of our time that Marxism is the chief conceptual alternative to liberal democracy and the political economy which is friendly to liberal democracy. The problems of democratic capitalism—and there are many problems—deserve a more worthy critique than Marxism offers. Yet it is the case that many Christians who would address the problems of capitalism, as Christians must, find themselves joining the Marxist side of the debate by default, as it were. Thus Marxist assumptions and, frequently, Marxist solutions are embraced by many Christians who sincerely take umbrage at being called Marxists.

Father Pedro Arrupe, former general superior of all Jesuits, addressed this phenomenon in a December 1980 letter to the order. He begins with the question: "Can a Christian, a Jesuit, adopt Marxist analysis as long as he distinguishes it from Marxist philosophy or ideology and also from Marxist praxis, at least considered in its totality?" He answers with a qualified negative, allowing that while it is just barely possible in theory it is almost always impossible in fact. In his carefully reasoned letter, Father Arrupe writes, "In brief, although Marxist analysis does not directly imply acceptance of Marxist philosophy as a whole—and still less of dialectical materialism as such—as it is normally understood it implies in fact a concept of human history which contradicts the Christian view of man and society and leads to strategies which threaten Christian values and attitudes." (*Catholic Mind,* September 81, pp. 59, 61-62.)

The witness of Pope John Paul, of Father Arrupe, and of others reflects a sober counterforce in Roman Catholicism to the Marxist inroads of recent years.

But to the extent that there are centers of teaching authority in mainline Protestantism, they are on economic questions dominated either by overt Marxists or by those who, willy nilly, have accepted the Marxist analysis of the failures of capitalism. In saying this, one is not making an accusation. It is simply a matter of taking people at their word, of doing them the courtesy of believing that they believe what they say they believe. For example, a recent statement of the World Council addresses the question of multinational or transnational corporations. It declares that transnationals "must be analyzed in the context of the world market system as a whole." "This system," the statement concludes, is "incompatible with our vision for a Just, Participatory and Sustainable Society." (*WCC Program on Churches and the TNCs*, pp. 24-5.)

It is very difficult to discuss these matters in a dispassionate manner. Many leaders in the Protestant mainline deeply resent having these questions raised. When statements such as those we have quoted are referred to, the frequent response is that they reflect "unrepresentative" or "marginal" viewpoints. But such a response is less than candid, I believe. These are not marginal views but reflect the controlling concepts within the church-and-society curias of mainline churches and their councils. One must appreciate keenly the fear of red-baiting. There is no denying that in the past it has happened that admirable efforts have been smeared by "McCarthyites" of the right. One has only to recall the civil rights movement under the leadership of Martin Luther King, Jr. But if we are to break through the

confusion, fear, and mendacity that envelop so much
religion-and-society debate today, it is imperative
that we recognize that fundamental issues are joined.
Oddly enough, we must try to persuade some religious leaders that the witness of the churches is more
important than they seem to think. For the sake of
religion and of religion's role in society, we must
begin to take what we say and what others say more
seriously.

To borrow a cliché from the social sciences, liberal
democracy and capitalism in particular are afflicted
by a legitimation crisis. Whatever the successes of
market economies in purely economic terms, it is
widely believed that the logic of capitalism is out of
synch with what, at least in the religious community,
are thought to be the normative moral metaphors.
Again, the opponents of democratic capitalism have
captured the moral rhetoric—of social justice, of
community, of self-sacrifice, of equality, and of compassion. The manipulation of these metaphors has
put capitalism on the defensive, not only in the view
of some radical moralists and third world agitators
but also in the self-understanding of many Christians
and Jews in the board rooms of American business.
The argument that capitalism "works" in strictly
economic terms is not sufficient. The defense of
democratic capitalism on purely pragmatic grounds
results in capitalism with a bad conscience. And the
argument that sundry socialisms have so obviously
failed, also in economic terms, is not persuasive to
those who insist that their brand of socialism has not
yet been tried.

A legitimation crisis has to do with ideas about

what is morally right. Such a crisis cannot be addressed effectively by people who are impatient with ideas. The story is told that Thomas Carlyle was once dining with a businessman who grew tired of Carlyle's loquacity and turned to him with the reproach, "Ideas, Mr. Carlyle, ideas, nothing but ideas!" To which Carlyle is said to have replied, "There was once a man named Rousseau who wrote a book containing nothing but ideas. The second edition was bound in the skins of those who laughed at the first." Unlike our apocalyptic friends, I do not suggest that the ideas currently being promulgated have brought us to the edge of cataclysmic change comparable to Rousseau's role in precipitating the French Revolution. I do suggest that ideas, and especially ideas about morality, will have a greater bearing upon the survival of democratic capitalism than anything the market is going to do tomorrow or in the next decade.

Contra the libertarians, it is not enough just to let the system work. Curiously enough, libertarian capitalists are the mirror image of their Marxist opponents when they declare, as some do, that once the correct economic system is established everything else will fall into place. Economic determinism of whatever stripe is, I believe, contrary to the way the world works. How the world works is of course eminently debatable. But, as a general proposition, I suggest that politics is a function of culture and at the heart of culture is religion. My thinking about economics is related to that general proposition. Lest there be any misunderstanding, by "religion" I mean those ultimate beliefs, whether or not they are

called religious, about how the world and our place
in it is and ought to be. For the vast majority of
Americans, of course, those ultimate beliefs are carried and articulated by Judaeo-Christian religion.

Economics, to be sure, is not the same thing as
culture and politics. As Michael Novak has recently
stressed, economics is a distinct sphere of human
activity. This, he and others contend, is one of the
great achievements of advanced societies—to have
established distinct spheres of operation for culture,
politics, and economics. In primitive societies, politics, culture, and economics are all of a piece. It is
one of the great psychological appeals of Marxism
that it promises, in the name of the future, to return
us to that primitive unitarianism of the social order.
While economics is a distinct sphere, it is not a separate sphere. Here we encounter the abiding
philosophical problem of how to distinguish without
separating and unite without confusing. The debate
today is in large part a debate between the separatists
and the confusionists.

Orthodox Marxists tell us that everything is finally
economics. Other voices, also in the churches, insist
that everything is finally political. I would not want
to be understood as saying that everything is finally
cultural. Against all those who express their monistic
hunger to "get it all together," we must be relentless
in pointing out that everything is not any one thing.
And yet everything is related to everything else,
however indirectly. Democratic capitalism could not
be experiencing a legitimation crisis were it not related to the culture. In this case, the relationship is
one of disharmony with the religiously based values

of the society which the political economy is to serve.

The problem has not gone unnoticed up till now. For many years figures such as Friedrich Hayek and Joseph Schumpeter have underscored the connections between economics, culture, and the imperiled future of freedom. More recently, thinkers such as Daniel Bell have analyzed "the cultural contradictions of capitalism." Robert Benne has made a significant contribution with his *The Ethic of Democratic Capitalism*. Peter Berger has taken up some of the issues relating to economic development and third world cultures, and of course I have already mentioned the work of Michael Novak. So we are witnessing what may be a new beginning in thinking through the legitimation crisis of the political economy in which we are all involved. The high promise of this new beginning is that it is premised upon the understanding that narrowly economic arguments are not enough. Surely people do need to be educated to the workings of "the wonderful bread machine," as capitalism has been called. But a more efficient bread machine does not meet the concerns of those who believe that man does not live by bread alone.

The task is not to provide a religious legitimation for one economic system or another, as though one or another is *the* Christian system. We can quote Bible passages at one another until the coming of the eschaton, and unfortunately some folks seem determined to do just that. The socialistically minded have no problem in finding passages in support of sharing the wealth, and latter-day Andrew Carnegies can find at least as many in support of the work ethic and the divinely ordained linkage between righteousness and prosperity. It is a futile exercise. In saying that, I do not mean to suggest that the scriptures are irrelevant to the present crisis. But the relevance of biblical religion is not discovered in the accumulation of Bible passages by fundamentalists of the left or of the right. The inspired writers knew nothing of the economic complexities of postindustrial societies. They did know that all social, political, and economic systems on this side of the Kingdom stand under the judgment of God.

Today liberation theologians make much of what is called the scriptural "option for the poor." Despite the questionable political uses to which the phrase is put, I believe that biblical religion does support an option for the poor. It is not a Marxist but a biblical insight that a society is judged along its fault lines, that we are judged by our relationship to the vulnerable, to the marginal, to those whom many view as expendable. That the defenders of market economies are so often and so manifestly uncomfortable with this insight has everything to do with the legitimation crisis of democratic capitalism. A more promising response is suggested by the work of P. T. Bauer, Theodore Schultz, Thomas Sowell, and some of the thinkers mentioned earlier. They contend that it is precisely for the sake of the poor and disadvantaged that the opportunities of market economics must be expanded. Alongside that argument, and tempering our dissatisfaction with its inadequacies, is another argument that needs to be advanced more vigorously, namely, that the alternative ways of political economy are not only economically disastrous but also invite one or another version of the Gulag Archipelago.

There is, I suggest, no authentically Christian argument for capitalism as such nor for socialism as such. There is an authentic and imperative Christian argument for human freedom. Especially is this true of religious freedom—or freedom of conscience, as some prefer. In this core assertion of the inviolable dignity of the person in relation to the absolute is grounded everything else we say about human rights. It is further true, I believe, that in the modern world human freedom and rights are protected only in those societies that can be described as liberal democracies. These are the considerations which precede and undergird what we might say about economics. The strongest case for capitalism is the case for freedom and for the democratic governance that makes freedom possible. Capitalism is not the sufficient cause of democratic freedom; there are societies claiming to be capitalist that are not free. Capitalism may not even be essential to democratic freedom, but no sober person can help but be impressed by the fact that nowhere in the world today is there democratic governance where it is not joined by a relatively free market economy. Nor can we fail to be impressed by the fact that those regimes which promise economic advance and equality at the price of freedom have, again and again, undermined economic advance, equality, and freedom alike.

Finally, it will not have escaped the reader's attention that the whole of this argument is a radical challenge to radical pluralism. It assumes values that are universal. In making this assumption, we are not "imposing our values" upon others. The claim, rather, is that we are calling others to recognize moral realities which are external to ourselves, which are imposed, as it were, upon all of us. One need not be a believer in divinely revealed truth in order to acknowledge the need for, and the possibility of, a shared universe of moral discourse. It is a great good fortune, however, that among believers today those most opposed to democratic capitalism still make their case in the moral terms of that universe of discourse. The legitimacy of capitalism will be more credible when its defenders liberate themselves from the limits of radical pluralism and join that moral debate.

PHILANTHROPY AS A RIGHT

by

Robert L. Payton

Robert L. Payton

Mr. Payton was appointed President of Exxon Education Foundation on March 1, 1977. He had earlier served as President of Hofstra University and C. W. Post College, and was U.S. Ambassador to the Federal Republic of Cameroon from 1967 to 1969.

Mr. Payton was on the staff of Washington University in St. Louis for nine years, serving as Vice Chancellor from 1961 to 1966. His earlier career included editorships of a weekly newspaper and a trade magazine. During World War II he served with the 11th Airborne Division.

Educated at the University of Chicago, from which he holds a master's degree, Mr. Payton was awarded an honorary doctor of literature degree by Adelphi University in 1975. He is also a Commander of the Order of the Bamoun Spider and officier of the Order of Valor of the United Republic of Cameroon.

A resident of Garden City, New York, Mr. Payton is a member of the Board of Technoserve, Inc., The Foundation Center, the International Council for Education Development, and the International Institute of Education.

PHILANTHROPY AS A RIGHT

by Robert L. Payton

These remarks grow out of two Cecil lectures: the first a more formal talk before the Rotary Club of Dallas on "Philanthropy and Freedom" and the second a much less formal seminar at The University of Texas at Dallas on "The Neglect of the Benign." I have since pursued these topics in a symposium sponsored by the Department of History at Hofstra University and in remarks to the University of Houston Foundation.

This preface is necessary because what follows is part of a process that began in 1981 with a presentation at the Woodrow Wilson International Center for Scholars in Washington, D.C., on "the future of philanthropy" and that continued with a Wilson Center symposium on "philanthropic values" in the fall of 1982. In sharing some of these thoughts with Andrew Cecil, it became apparent that there is a deep compatibility between his interest in the moral values of a free society and my interest in the philanthropic tradition in America.

This essay, then, marks one stage in the development of one person's thought about philanthropy. Thinking about philanthropy usually begins with being asked to give money for a "good cause" and then moves to asking others to give their money for a (perhaps different) good cause. All Americans participate in the first stage of the process; it is not possible to live in this society and not be asked incessantly to give money for good causes.

There is, of course, great difference of opinion as to what constitutes a good cause; there is a cause to delight and offend every taste.

Many of the activities that are alleged to be good causes would change the economy, reform our morals, liberate our children, rescue the poor, decorate our museums, correct our spelling. Although some of these causes are arguably trivial and inconsequential, some of them are directly related to our foundations as a society.

Even so, even with the extraordinary visibility of philanthropy in our lives, even with the seismic disturbances that philanthropically supported activities sometimes cause, it is a nonsubject in academic terms. It is not taught, except as a technique for practitioners, in American colleges and universities.

This is the argument: Philanthropy permeates American life, touches each one of us countless times in countless ways; philanthropy provides the resources for some of the most important activities that give shape and substance to our efforts to be a free and open and democratic society, and yet, inexplicably, it is not a matter of central intellectual concern, of thought and study.

Some definitions are in order before going further. Our usage is casual in talking about these subjects, and there is not an available glossary of terms to which we can all turn confidently for reference. "Philanthropy" is used here as an umbrella-term to cover all types of private giving for public purposes.

(In the background is the original sense of "love of mankind," a generalized benevolence, but philanthropy has come to represent that more limited expression of concern for others as manifested in gifts of money: "one-way transfers of exchangeables.")

There are two broad objectives served by gifts of money for public purposes, one originating in the Judaeo-Christian tradition and the other having its earliest expression classical Greece. *Charity* is the word we use to describe gifts that are intended to relieve suffering, to be personal acts of mercy to others in distress who are beyond our own clear realm of responsibility. Charitable concern, in that sense, is at the heart of most of our voluntary giving.

The word *philanthropy,* on the other hand, comes to us from the Greeks and Romans, where most of our ideas about political society originated. Although there is evidence of a charitable concern in classical civilization, the predominant thrust of giving is to improve the life of the community. Philanthropy also tends to signify larger gifts, more carefully rationalized, less personal and spontaneous, more directed toward the future.

I have found it helpful to think of charity and philanthropy as analogous to the ideas of "relief" and "development" in foreign aid. (That context also provides a more dramatic reminder of the choices involved in giving, the sometimes agonizing trade-offs between the relief of suffering today and the prevention of suffering tomorrow.)

If we set aside the small amount of giving for public purposes that takes place between individuals and concentrate on the vast majority of giving that is done to and through organizations and institutions, we have to bring into the discussion of philanthropy the recipients of our giving. These are corporate entities that have special status in our society, status established by law and greatly encouraged by public policy.

I speak now of what is called the "independent sector," the vast collection of organizations that operate on a not-for-profit basis and for public rather than private purposes. These organizations are private in terms of their control, and voluntary in terms of their participation. Any financial surplus that may on occasion be generated by their activities is not distributed as profits for the private benefit of the "owners."

The independent sector, then, is not part of the marketplace because the exchange that takes place is one-way and not for profit, and it is not an instrument of government because it depends on voluntary action and has no police power or taxing authority.

Within the scope of the independent sector are all those organized activities that have to do with private gifts for public purposes—that is, with philanthropy. The scope of the independent sector and of philanthropy constitutes the first part of the essay that follows. The second part attempts to discuss the role of the independent sector and of philanthropy in defining and advancing the moral values of the free society. The third part then examines the place of the independent sector and of philanthropy in the higher educational system, on the assumption that it is important to consider the way philanthropy is treated in education and what confidence we should have in the continuation of that tradition.

The Independent Sector

Under the term "independent sector," we will find "all voluntary organizations, churches, schools, private foundations, and the social responsibility programs of corporations that engage in charitable, educational, religious, scientific, and other not-for-profit activities that serve the public good."

In 1982 it is estimated that there were 793,000 organizations in the independent sector, 339,000 of which were churches. (The statistics in this paragraph and following are drawn from the *Fact Book* to be published in spring 1984 by Independent Sector, organized and edited by Virginia A. Hodgkinson.) To put those numbers in some perspective, were one to count all of the "operating entities" in the United States, one would find 16.8 million business organizations and 1.2 million not-for-profit organizations. (The not-for-profit organizations include about 400,000 that are for the benefit of their members, such as veterans organizations and mutual aid associations; these organizations, plus the approximately 800,000 independent sector organizations, make up the "not-for-profit" sector.)

Employment in the independent sector was 10.2 million people, 6.1 million of whom were full-time or part-time employees. (The remaining 4.1 million represent the conversion of volunteer time to a "full-time equivalent" number.) These and other volunteers—80 million of them—contribute 8.4 billion hours of work to American society. That is estimated to be the equivalent of 4.9 million full-time employees—or the equivalent of $63 billion of financially uncompensated services.

The independent sector thus represents about 6 percent of national income (business contributes 80 percent and government 14 percent):

"In 1972 constant dollars, the not-for-profit organizations expended $200 in 1960 and $340 in 1982 for every American. Of these expenditures, it is estimated that over 90 percent of this contribution came from the independent sector."

Independent sector organizations in 1980 accounted for 9.2 percent of all employment and 8.2 percent of all earnings from labor.

Philanthropy, as the part of the independent sector that is concerned with gifts of money, reveals this profile:

- An estimated 86 percent of all Americans 18 and over contribute to at least one charitable organization.
- The average philanthropic contribution in 1981 was $475.
- The total amount contributed in 1982 was $60.4 billion.
- Sources:
Individuals	$48.7 billion	80.7%
Bequests	5.5	9.0
Foundations	3.2	5.2
Corporations	3.1	5.1
- Recipients:
Religion	$28.1	46.5%
Education	8.6	14.2
Health	8.4	13.9
Social Welfare	6.3	10.5

Arts-Humanities	5.0	8.2
Civic and Public	1.7	2.8
Other	2.4	3.9

(This table is from *Giving USA–1983 Annual Report*, published by the Association of Fund Raising Counsel in New York.)

Higher education reported voluntary support totalling $4.9 billion in 1981-1982. Of that, 26 percent came from alumni, 23 percent from nonalumni, 21 percent from foundations, and 20 percent from corporations.

These figures are intended to support the contention that philanthropy permeates American life, both in terms of giving and in terms of the vast array of voluntary service it supports.

That is my first point.

Philanthropy and Freedom

My second point is that philanthropy is essential to our efforts to make this a free, open, and democratic society. Robert Bremner's book, *American Philanthropy*, provides a summary of the role of philanthropy in American history. It touches on the philanthropic establishment of most of the educational, cultural, social, and religious institutions of the society. It refers to the vast array of efforts to reform and improve the society and to relieve suffering. Let me offer some contemporary examples, chosen at random from direct mail fund-raising appeals:

- New York Association for the Blind
- Meals for Millions/Freedom from Hunger Foundation
- Arthritis Foundation
- Prision Fellowship
- Community Service Society of New York
- The Fire Island Lighthouse Preservation Society
- The University of Chicago
- The Ad Hoc Committee in Defense of Life
- Hunger Action Coordination
- USOCA (US Out of Central America)
- Union of Councils of Soviet Jews

All of these organizations are private—that is, not under direct government control—and tax-exempt—that is, determined by the Internal Revenue Service to operate in the public interest. Contributions to these organizations are considered to be tax deductible. Altough often concerned with public issues and policies, these organizations are not defined as "political." Some of them compete with for-profit business, but they are still treated as not-for-profit (because any surpluses are not distributed to their "owners") and as in the public interest. To be classified as acting in the public interest means that these organizations relieve the public tax effort that might otherwise be undertaken to provide funds for these services.

This use of tax policy and other legislation to encourage private sector giving and voluntary service results in a vast and influential system. It is a system

that is unique in the world. Charles Livingston-
Booth, President of the International Standing Conference on Philanthropy, pointed this out recently in
his remarks at a conference in New York. In the
Scandinavian countries, he noted, "taxation provides a disincentive to giving." "In Belgium a newly
arrived American multinational offered a swimming
pool to the local community, which was angrily refused on the grounds that this is a proper responsibility of government and no such interference would
be tolerated." Japan has but twenty foundations
(compared to some 22,000 in the United States). In
France, government permission is required to make
a significant gift to charity. In Finland, one of the
many countries to limit the portion of one's private
estate that can be left to charity, "the only giving that
attracts tax privileges is to a body providing national
defense."

The contrasting diversity of American philanthropy is worth mentioning again:

- Amnesty International
- New York Public Library
- The Committee for a Sane Nuclear Policy
- Catholic Relief Services

Or take this list, from the early part of the century,
from Bremner's *American Philanthropy:* ·

"Churches, home and foreign missions, temper-
ance organizations . . . orphanages, and homes for
the aged . . . the plight of newsboys, working
girls, distressed immigrants, tenement dwellers,
and southern mountain children . . ." (University
of Chicago Press, 1960, pp. 122-123).

The list is almost endless: YMCA, YWCA, YMHA, Salvation Army, Volunteers of America, Boy Scouts, Girl Scouts, Campfire Girls, National Tuberculosis Association, American Cancer Society, Goodwill Industries, The Lighthouse, NAACP, Urban League, American Association of Labor Legislation, National Child Labor Committee . . .

In the United States, one could review instructively the legal history of the *right* to organize voluntarily for public purposes, the *right* to raise money, and the *right* to give it for public purposes. It is a constitutional history that supports the legislative actions to encourage voluntary service and philanthropy by tax policy. From the earliest days, it also reflects public and private sector cooperation, private giving supplementing and stimulating public funds.

Neglect of the Benign

My argument thus far has been intended to provide a quantitative outline of philanthropy and a qualitative sketch of some of the purposes it serves, purposes that I contend are central to our efforts to be a free, open, and democratic society. All of those organizations come into being, and call upon voluntary giving, because the operations of government and its bureaucracies, of the marketplace and its business enterprises, fall short of perfection. In the minds of some people, there is need for charitable acts to relieve suffering beyond what the system seems able to provide and need for philanthropic improvements of the community.

One might then conclude, as I have, that philanthropy, especially when considered in its broader implications, is an activity of substantial importance. It is a subject worthy of scholarly research, research that could then be utilized in programs of education and training. What one finds, however, is a very uneven record of scholarship from one field of study to another, often superficial training programs, and a total neglect of the subject as a topic in undergraduate general education.

Let me deal first with scholarly research. The two fields that seem to have devoted the most significant energy to the subject are history and social work. Barry Karl of the University of Chicago and Stanley Katz of Princeton University are engaged in a two-volume history of the impact of philanthropy on public policy in twentieth-century America. Bremner's *American Philanthropy*, a really excellent introductory survey written in 1960 for the University of Chicago Press series in the history of American civilization, has been reprinted recently but without revision.

The best new book that I have seen is by James Douglas, a British political scientist now teaching at Northwestern University *(Why Charity? The Case for a Third Sector*, Sage Publications, Inc., 1983). Douglas addresses the reasons why a third sector of private philanthropy and voluntary service exists in the first place: He analyzes the constraints and the limitations on government and the marketplace. Economics does not seem to have provided a satisfactory solution to what Russell Hardin calls "the back of the invisible hand" or for the paradox of public goods. An economist has asked whether charity must not be coerced—that is, whether the basic human needs met by voluntary charity must not instead be provided by government allocation.

There is also a valuable new anthology on *America's Voluntary Spirit* (The Foundation Center, 1983), edited by Brian O'Connell, who also serves as President of the organization called Independent Sector.

Training tends to be found in programs for managers of not-for-profit organizations or in courses in fund-raising. The only systematic degree training that deals with philanthropy in depth is in social work, although some business schools address it in courses in corporate social responsibility.

Let me illustrate my point about the neglect of philanthropy in general education by referring to recent course catalogues of Amherst College, The University of Texas at Dallas, and Hofstra University. To the best of my knowledge, none of these catalogues lists courses making any reference to charity or philanthropy or the independent sector.

Amherst offers an Economics course entitled "Radical Perspectives on Capitalism" that does not, according to the hundred words or so of summary description in the 1980-81 catalogue, make mention of charity or philanthropy, even to repudiate them. Course 20, "Economics and Property Rights," discussses "the use of common property resources . . . the historical development of private property and its regulation . . . contracts, and the relationships between property, equity, individual freedom and the public interest," but apparently with no reference to philanthropy and the right to donate private property for public purposes. Political Science 21, "American Government," makes reference to "the relationship of private aspirations and public norms," and Political Science 23, "Political Obligations," mentions "the obligation to rescue." Political Science 24, "Politics in Third World Nations," declares that "special attention will be paid to the problems of human rights and world hunger." Is there reference in these courses to the work, say, of the Medical Mission Sisters? To CARE? To Bread for the World? To the impact of philanthropy on American foreign policy?

There are no courses listed on the literature of charity at Amherst, but there is a course on the literature of madness.

Amherst, by the way, was founded in 1821. The historian Merle Curti describes its origins: "Canvassing the small towns of western Massachusetts, the representatives of Amherst's 'Charity Fund,' as it was known, were remarkably successful. In less than a year they raised $37,000 from 274 individuals for most of whom philanthropy of any amount was a sacrifice." (Merle Curti and Roderick Nash, *Philanthropy in the Shaping of American Higher Education*, Rutgers University Press, 1965, p. 46.) Amherst has developed to the point where it proudly reports endowments for student aid amounting to more than $6 million—enough from past giving to permit a policy that no student will be denied admission on the basis of financial need alone.

The only other reference to philanthropy that I could find in the Amherst catalogue was a bibliographic reference to the interesting little book, *Doing Good: The Limits of Benevolence,* mentioned among a dozen other titles in an interdisciplinary course on "Perspectives on the Professions." That reference touches, at least, on what I have in mind: introducing the idea of philanthropy into courses of general education that violate the sacred precincts of the specialized disciplines.

As far as I have been able to discover, philanthropy is no more a part of the education of undergraduates at Hofstra than it is elsewhere. Social Psychology 159 probably does not deal with dominance and dependency as an aspect of giving and receiving charity. Social and Political Philosophy 4 probably does not give much time to philanthropy, and Introduction to Ethics II probably does not use philanthropy to illustrate the discussion of "ethical progress." English 132 on the nineteenth-century British novel probably does not use Dickens' satirical attack on charity as practiced in his time as an illustration of the literature of charity. Political Science 105 on "Public Policy in the United States" probably does not reveal to students the extraordinary role played by philanthropy and the independent sector in shaping American public policy. (This is an oversight that might well be remedied when the historians Karl and Katz publish the history mentioned earlier.)

The University of Texas at Dallas is a public institution, upper division and graduate only. It occupies space largely provided by individuals associated with Texas Instruments Incorporated and by the corporation itself, people like Eugene McDermott and Erik Jonsson in particular.

There is a course at UT-Dallas in "The Ethical Conduct of Business" and another in "Corporations and Politics," but neither course description makes explicit reference to the growing role of the corporation in philanthropy or to the relationship of corporate philanthropy to the formation of public policy. Presumably one turns instead to History 3366, "Themes in the Social History of the United States: Race, Class, Sex, and Social Change," "a survey of social history, focusing on the American experience ... [that] fulfills one-half of the Texas legislative requirement for six hours in American history." (It may also indicate what you get when the legislature takes it upon itself to tell faculty members what to teach.)

I am necessarily tentative in all these sweeping statements about what is taught about philanthropy to undergraduates, for I have based what I say merely on the examination of course catalogues and course descriptions and on the indexes of college textbooks. I welcome evidence that would correct my impression that philanthropy is simply ignored in the American college classroom.

My argument has been that philanthropy operates on such an enormous scale and is so widely diffused in American life that it seems astonishing that it has failed to capture the attention of the academic community in the United States. Philanthropy and voluntary service broadly considered are, in my opinion, vital to the preservation of freedom, but their operation and purpose and place in our tradition must be taught and studied and learned if they are to survive. They are, at the moment, not a system of thought but a confusion of law and custom and attitude and behavior and organization—and simply ignorance. Offering such intellectual disarray holds out little promise for effective response to other, competing systems.

One faculty member (a social historian) remarked that "If we did teach about philanthropy you probably wouldn't like what we taught." Similar arguments bring out a point of view that sees charity as demeaning to the recipients and philanthropy either as a means of keeping the poor in their place or for diverting tax monies to the cultural priorities of the rich. Corporate giving, in this view, is rejected on the grounds that it only serves to strengthen an already insidious capitalist influence.

A contrasting position, still widely held by skeptics in the business community, is that corporations should leave philanthropy to individuals; they hold the nineteenth-century opinion that "charity has no place at the board table." Libertarians, more visible these days if not more numerous, give such high priority to individualism that they are suspicious of all social action proposed under the rubric of benevolence.

Let me contrast the neglect of philanthropy with the systematic attention paid to a contrasting set of values. *The Left Academy,* edited by Edward Vernoff and the well-known, self-described Marxist political-scientist Bertell Ollman, published in 1982 by McGraw-Hill, is a discipline-by-discipline report on the status of the "Marxist perspective" on American campuses. Thirty years ago such a book title would have signalled an exposé written by a fervent

anticommunist and read eagerly by members of such
organizations as the John Birch Society. Today it is
published—and reprinted—by a mainstream pub-
lishing house and read by mainstream academics as
well as by those who think of themselves as Marxists.

"A Marxist cultural revolution is taking place
today in American universities," say the editors in
their introduction. They go on to report the publication of "four Marxist-inspired textbooks in American
government" and the publication of "over fifteen
books on Marx and Marxism" by Oxford, Cambridge,
and Princeton university presses. (*The Left
Academy*, page 1.)

"There are over 400 courses given today in Marxist
philosophy . . ." according to Ollman and Vernoff.
The popularity of Marxist teaching innovations is not
my point, however; the point is the absence of
teaching about the tradition of voluntary service and
private giving in American life. It does indeed make
a difference to one's thought about the American
system whether one sees it through eyes that legitimate philanthropy or through eyes that see legitimacy only in the state. Quite apart from opinions of
the kind I have been describing (and expressing),
philanthropy as it is organized in the United States
provides the means for social change that is an interesting alternative to those to which other, especially Marxist, societies are limited.

Philanthropy is a subject that touches the life of
every student and every faculty member at every
American college. It is easily related to every discipline of the humanities and social sciences and to
professional studies like medicine, law, and busi-

ness. It *could* be taught, and in my opinion it *should* be taught, but it is not taught.

Conclusion

The system of charity and philanthropy and voluntary service is at work in almost every aspect of our lives. We give to it and we receive from it. We use it to help others and to express our ideas about how life could be made better for all of us.

The independent sector provides a means by which we can make corrections in the way our economic, political, and social systems work. The device permits peaceful change, constantly under way, of an infinite plurality and complexity—as diverse as we are ourselves as a free, open, and democratic society.

There is reason for the concern that this complex and rich tradition will not thrive without care and encouragement and understanding. Highly organized and powerfully funded alternative ideologies are pressing upon us; we might by default find our system modified significantly while we are not attending to it. Technical adjustments might be made in tax policy, in the law regulating not-for-profit organizations, in the definitions of which organizations are eligible for tax exemption and of which gifts are eligible for tax deduction, in the boundaries surrounding corporate contributions, or in the practices of endowed foundations.

The Andrew R. Cecil Lectures on Moral Values in a Free Society is a proper context within which to raise such questions and to express such concerns. The lecturers in this series share strong convictions

about the importance of public discourse that respects our tradition without insisting on blind allegiance to it. Public discourse about the issues that
unite and divide us owes much to the right to raise
money and the right to give it.

No other society has been so bold in granting that
right and in extending its use. Perhaps no other society is so free.

CONSTITUTIONAL LIBERTY IN WESTERN CIVILIZATION: THE AMERICAN REPUBLIC

by

Peter J. Stanlis

Peter J. Stanlis

Professor Stanlis, a native of New Jersey, took his B.A. at Middlebury Colege (1942), his M.A. at the Bread Loaf School of English (1944), and his Ph.D. at the University of Michigan (1951). He has taught at a number of colleges and universities, and since 1968 has been at Rockford College, Rockford, Illinois, where he was appointed Distinguished Professor of Humanities in 1974.

Professor Stanlis has published numerous articles on political, historical, and legal subjects, and a pioneer study in government, A Methodology for Studying the Services of Local Government. *His principal academic specialty has been eighteenth-century literature, and he has written and edited many studies of Edmund Burke, ranging from* Edmund Burke and the Natural Law (1958) *to* Edmund Burke: A Bibliography of Secondary Studies to 1982 *(with Clara I. Gandy, 1983). He has also written extensively on Robert Frost.*

The recipient of numerous grants and writing awards, Professor Stanlis is a member of many professional organizations including the Johnson Society of the Great Lakes Region, of which he was President in 1964-1965. He is a co-founder of the American Society for Eighteenth Century Studies.

In the realm of public service, Professor Stanlis has served extensively in local government and was a member of the Constitutional Revision Commission of the State of Michigan. President Reagan appointed him to a six-year term on the National Council of the Humanities in 1982.

CONSTITUTIONAL LIBERTY IN WESTERN CIVILIZATION: THE AMERICAN REPUBLIC

by Peter J. Stanlis

Preface

My subject is constitutional liberty, and particularly the contribution to constitutional liberty in Western civilization of the American republic. I shall be more concerned with the interaction between theory and practical life than with pure theory. I shall not treat constitutional liberty as an abstract theoretical concept derived speculatively from rational premises, without roots in history, as from some supposed primitive "state of nature" prior to the existence of organized civil society. History does not record any nation that ever originated through a "social contract" out of a supposed "state of nature," such as was posited by Thomas Hobbes (1588-1679), John Locke (1632-1704), and Jean-Jacques Rousseau (1712-1778). I believe that discussions of the American republic are flawed from the start when they are based upon seventeenth- and eighteenth-century theories of a "social contract," rather than upon the total culture of Western civilization within recorded history. Such studies constitute a fictional fairyland of political theory. Neither a Hobbist jungle-like hypothetical "state of nature," nor a Lockean Eden-like supposedly historical "state of nature," nor an

ambiguous Rousseauistic idyllic "state of nature"
can provide an adequate basis for understanding the
American republic. Even when scholars who accept
these writers' premises include an historical dimension in their studies by treating the American constitution as a representative document of the "Enlightenment," their historic base is far too narrow
and limited.

Rather than such speculative ideological writers as
Hobbes, Locke, and Rousseau, I take for my models
such historically-oriented writers on constitutional
liberty as Montesquieu (1689-1755), Edmund Burke
(1729-1797), and Lord Acton (1834-1902). American
constitutional liberty is the concrete product of empirical history, an entailed inheritance from our
European and American ancestors, the hard-won result of heroic efforts by many men over many centuries, in actions of war and peace. These men sought
to establish, maintain, or transmit the practical principles of individual and social freedom that from at
least the fifth century B.C. in Greece had gradually
become embodied as norms in the doctrines of religion and principles of philosophy, in moral laws, in
systems of law, and in the customs and manners of
the nations which created the traditions of Western
civilization.

In the two decades between 1870-1890, when
Lord Acton proposed to write *The History of Liberty*
from Classical antiquity to 1880, he estimated that it
would take 50,000 pages to describe the slow and
uneven growth of constitutional liberty in Western
civilization. (See *Letters of Acton to Mary
Gladstone*, London, 1913, p. 101.) Although Acton

abandoned his project and it became known as "the greatest book that was never written," he nevertheless summarized how history revealed the means of securing constitutional liberty and its social ends:

> "The acquisition of real definite freedom is a very slow and tardy process. These liberties are the product of a long conflict with absolutism, and of a gradual development, which by establishing definite rights revives in positive form the negative liberty of an unformed society. The object and the result of this process is the organization of self-government, the substitution of right for force, of authority for power, of duty for necessity and of a moral for a physical relation between government and people." (Acton, "Mr. Goldwin Smith's Irish History," in *History of Freedom,* pp. 252-253.)

Acton believed that the Founding Fathers of the American republic, in framing and adopting the federal Constitution, left some serious problems unsolved, yet they extended the principles of civil freedom beyond any previous achievement in Western civilization:

> "The Americans proceeded to give themselves a Constitution which should hold them together more effectively than the Congress which carried them through the war, and they held a Convention for the purpose at Philadelphia during the summer of 1787. The difficulty was to find terms of union between the three great states— Virginia, Pennsylvania, Massachusetts—and the smaller ones. . . . The great states would not allow

equal power to the others; the small ones would not allow themselves to be swamped by mere numbers. Therefore one chamber was given to population, and the other, the Senate, to the states on equal terms. Every citizen was made subject to the federal government as well as to that of his own state. The powers of the states were limited. The powers of the federal government were actually enumerated, and thus the states and the union were a check on each other. That principle of division was the most efficacious restraint on democracy that has been devised; for the temper of the Constitutional Convention was as conservative as the Declaration of Independence was revolutionary.

"The Federal Constitution did not deal with the question of religious liberty. The rules for the election of the president and for that of the vice-president proved a failure. Slavery was deplored, was denounced, and was retained. The absence of a definition of State Rights led to the most sanguinary civil war of modern times. . . . And yet, by the development of the principle of Federalism, it has produced a community more powerful, more prosperous, more intelligent, and more free than any other which the world has seen." (Acton, "The American Revolution," in *Lectures on Modern History,* London, 1912, p. 314.)

The American republic today is much more than the sum total of its formal establishment late in the eighteenth century, and its subsequent history; its historical origins and its religious, legal, and philosophical foundations must be perceived in terms of the whole culture of Western civilization during at least the past 2,500 years.

American constitutional liberty needs to be defined not in abstract ideological terms, but through an awareness of its total historical origins and development in Europe—through religious and moral laws, legal systems such as the Justinian Code and English common law, social customs, and the structure and function of basic institutions, and their relationship to each other and to individuals, and to these individuals' rights and duties as human beings and as citizens of a particular state or nation. Rather than a precivil "state of nature" and "social contract," I assume Aristotle's precept that "the state is a creation of nature, and that man is by nature a political animal." (Aristotle, *Politics*, trans. Benjamin Jowett, Bk. I, Ch. 2, in *The Basic Works of Aristotle*, Ed. Richard McKeon, New York, 1941, p. 1129.) Even within the empirical frame of reference provided by history, definitions of liberty are notoriously inadequate, and fail to do justice to the complexities of any constitutional system, or the essential nature of liberty. As Edmund Burke said on this subject:

"Of all the loose terms in the world, liberty is the most indefinite. It is not solitary, unconnected, individual, selfish liberty, as if every man was to regulate the whole of his conduct by his own will. The liberty I mean is *social* freedom. It is that state of things in which liberty is secured by the equality of restraint. A constitution of things in which the liberty of no one man, and no body of men, and no number of men, can find means to trespass on the liberty of any person, or any description of persons, in the society. This kind of liberty is, indeed, but another name for justice; ascertained by wise laws, and secured by well-constructed institutions." (Burke, "A Letter to M. Depont," in *Selected Writings and Speeches,* Ed. Peter J. Stanlis, Garden City, New York, 1963, p. 420.)

Burke's conception of civil liberty is corporate, within institutionally organized society, subject to moral and legal restraints, and ascertainable within European history.

To comprehend American constitutional liberty in terms of Burke's definition, within Western civilization, we would have to note the extent to which every European society and its total culture contributed to the principles and values which ultimately were incorporated into American society and its republican constitution. Had we but world enough and time we might draw out a few threads in the grand fabric of liberty which Lord Acton proposed to weave. But in this limited discussion we cannot do more than identify a few of the more vital contributions to liberty made by the ancient Israelites, Greeks, and Romans, by Medieval Christianity, and during the so-called Renaissance and Enlightenment periods of European history. Over the centuries history provides the most concrete empirical evidence of the dynamic embodiment in human affairs of the normative moral and legal principles of constitutional liberty. As a succession of sensory archetypal frames in a familiar social landscape, crucial events in Western civilization comprise a continuous cinematic image, unfolding through past time toward the contemporary moment and scene. For those who have the true historical sense, the sense of the pastness of the past and of its living presence, time is more relative in history than in physics, because vital historical events never die. Events in past time which affect us constantly today, though we are unaware of them, are as alive in us as our own self-generated thoughts and feelings, and often provide those unquestioned premises that shape our lives.

Liberty in the Ancient World: Israel, Greece, and Rome

Any summary of the contribution to political liberty of the ancient Israelites, who evolved from the Hebrews, may well begin with the monotheistic conception of God put forth by their lawgiver, Moses: "Hear O Israel: the Lord our God, the Lord is One." (*Deuteronomy* 6:4-9.) The one true and personal God of Abraham, Isaac, and Jacob, called "Yahweh" (Jehovah), meaning "He who is," at once transcendent and existentially immanent, not discovered by reason or research ("Canst thou by searching find our God?", Job 11:7), but revealed to God's own chosen people through such prophets as Amos, Jeremiah, Micah, Nathan, Isaiah, Ezekiel, and Moses, provided the whole basis of liberty to the Israelites, both within each separate soul and in their corporate society. The supremacy of the revealed moral law in the Decalogue implied a patriarchal covenant between God and His people, between the rulers of Israel and the people, and among the people themselves. Their religious covenant was far more inclusive than any theories of a social contract, as set forth by Hobbes, Locke, or Rousseau, because it permeated and fused into an indistinguishable unity their whole history; their myths, legends, and poetry; their politics and religion; and their sense of destiny as a people. The Bible—by far the most influential book in Western civilization—makes it clear that their covenant with God includes a doctrine of the divine right and duty of kings, such as governed their society under their ordained monarchs, Saul, David (ruled from 1005-965 B.C.), and his son Solomon (ruled from 965-925 B.C.). The covenant of God and Israel incorporated into the concept of political liberty the ultimate absolute primacy of the individual conscience, informed by moral law. To fulfill their divine covenant was considered their greatest achievement, as sainthood was for Christians, and that which assured each individual his salvation. The Israelite doctrine of the covenant makes each individual soul supremely important and of equal value to God and provides the ethical basis for the concept of equality under the law, a fundamental principle of constitutional government. The doctrine of the covenant also establishes a providential view of history, wholly distinct from the pagan classical conception of history as a temporal cycle of events and from the modern secular theory of history as progress. To an Israelite the monotheistic conception of God and the covenant provided a meaning for life within the temporal processes of history, but also beyond history in the personal immortality of the soul through religion.

Since the people possessed sovereign rights under the revealed law, the power of the Kings of Israel, as shepherds of the people responsible to God, was limited by the laws of the Torah. (See *Deuteronomy* 17:14-20.) The kings held their power in trust and were obliged to respect the liberty and private property of their subjects. Like all of their ancient neighbors the Israelites permitted slavery, with qualifications, as part of their legal system, a fact which centuries later enabled European and American Christians to claim a biblical sanction for slavery.

The Israelites were also probably the first people to have a deep social consciousness regarding the plight of people living in poverty. Beginning with the prophet Amos, the prophets of Israel showed a profound concern about injustice and oppression against the poor and the indifference of rulers toward the poor. The Old Testament prophets were not engaged in social revolution, but were appealing to the conscience of rulers to live up to the covenant. The prophets reminded the powerful and the rich that it was their moral duty, and not an optional choice, to show charity for the poor. Twenty centuries before John Locke defended the rights of freeholders as a basic duty of government, the Israelites defended the rights of private property as a fundamental principle of justice and liberty. But they insisted that justice in property and wealth had to be combined with mercy to the poor.

The common view of many modern scholars that the law of the Old Testament is concerned with justice whereas the New Testament is concerned with mercy is both unhistorical and invalid. This in-

terpretation stresses the role of Moses as lawgiver
too much, and erroneously makes Christ's Sermon
on the Mount a complete break with the Jewish tradition. In truth, both the Old and the New Testa-
ments are concerned with both justice and mercy. To
separate justice and mercy and to make mercy for the
poor the main or only concern of the moral law is to
become what Robert Frost once called "a New Testament saphead." (For Frost's dramatic treatment of
the justice-mercy contradiction, see his two poetic
dramas, *A Masque of Reason* [1945] and *A Masque of
Mercy* [1947].) Once the harmony of justice and
mercy was destroyed, the way was opened for the
triumph of modern socialism, from its mildest forms
in social welfare to the most revolutionary collec-
tivism of Communism. Socialism has been well described as a secular heresy from the Judaeo-
Christian religious tradition. The socialist solution to
the problem of poverty is to exploit the envy of the
poor and the pride of the rich, to create class warfare,
to separate justice from mercy, and to make mercy to
the poor the greatest social virtue. With socialists, in
theory if not in practice, the test of a society is always
the treatment of the poor. Under socialism mercy to
the poor often takes the form of injustice to the rich.
Mild forms of socialism are evident in practically
every modern nation, in the leveling devices of
graduated income taxes and other methods to bring
about redistribution of wealth and establish equality
of economic condition. Communism, as the most extreme form of socialism, considers it an act of justice
to confiscate the wealth of the rich, to eliminate all
private property, to nationalize industry, to collec-

tivize farms through "land reforms," and to give the
one-party totalitarian State a complete monopoly of
power over the people. It is a sign of how confused
modern men are, even in democratic societies, that
the redistribution of wealth by the State is called
"distributive justice" rather than mercy to the poor.
To the extent that the modern secular State has di-
gressed from the balanced harmony between justice
and mercy held by the ancient Israelites, the principles of liberty (which depend upon the protection of
private property), and the harmony of rich and poor
in society, have been greatly weakened.

If Israel provided some basic religious normative
principles for liberty in Western civilization, the ancient Greeks furnished the philosophical norms for
civic freedom through culture. Whereas the Israelites were God's chosen people, the Athenian Greeks
were the culturally elect, a free people who perceived non-Hellenic peoples as "barbarians." The
leaders and lawgivers of the Greeks were not priests,
nor prophets such as Moses, dealing in divine mys-
teries, but statesmen such as Pericles, Solon, and
Lycurgus and philosophers such as Socrates, Plato,
and Aristotle, who used highly empirical and rational methods to explain external nature and human
society through science and philosophy. Their complex mythology provided them with a convenient
means of defining through symbols the relationships
between the gods, man, and physical nature. From
Thales to Socrates, Greek philosophy was centered
in physical nature; after Socrates their main concern
was not with the cosmos but with human nature and
civil society, with the problems of justice, order,

individual freedom, and the place of art in society. In shifting attention from the "macrocosm" of the physical universe and the "harmony of the spheres" to the "microcosm" of man and the harmony of civil society, the Greeks made the inner perfection of human nature in society the great end of man. This alone was an enormous contribution to liberty in Western civilization. The great aphorism of Greek Socratic philosophy, "Know thyself," marked the beginning of intellectual freedom and self-knowledge, an essential requisite for moral and political liberty, both for individuals and society.

Before Greek philosphers could define the essential principles of a constitutionally just and free society, the social and political organization of Greek society had to be developed to a high degree of perfection. The supreme form of organized Greek society was the city-state, or *polis*, which Eric Voegelin noted "began with Solon . . . and came to a close with Cleophon, toward the end of the Peloponnesian War." (Eric Voegelin, *Order and History: The World of the Polis*, Baton Rouge, La., 1957, p. 120.) Whether oligarchic, aristocratic, or democratic, the *polis* was an independent and self-sufficient citadel of close blood relationships, which grew into a free community unified by the common and combined attributes of a family, tribe, city, province, state, or nation. Those city-states which founded colonies around the Mediterranean Sea added the dimension of empire, but without any imperial bureaucracy or centralization of authority. The world of the *polis* always remained a loose aggregation of independent sovereign city-states, with sovereignty on the local level, and never became a federated or united Hellenic nation. This was a great asset to individual liberty, but proved fatal for the survival of Greek civilization against foreign enemies. Although the Greek *polis* included slavery, its free citizens enjoyed all the rights and privileges of constitutional liberty under a well-organized state, in both their private and communal lives, often beyond class conflicts.

The ordered freedom of the Greek *polis* reached its highest fulfillment in Athens under Pericles (490?-429 B.C.), when Greek culture and democratic freedom rose to unparalled heights. The political origins of constitutional liberty in Western civilization have their genesis during the Periclean age. Within one century, in an Athens whose population probably never exceeded 100,000 people, there occurred an almost incredible outpouring of the free creative spirit of man, which produced some of the world's greatest artists, dramatists, philosophers, statesmen, and historians. Earlier, from around the eighth century B.C., the most perceptive insights into Greek thought and culture were revealed in Homer's *Iliad* and *Odyssey*. Until the time of Plato, these epics provided the whole basis of Greek education, art, and religion. Beyond Homer the Greek contribution to the culture and liberty of Western civilization includes Hesiod's *Works and Days;* the fragments from the Milesian philosophers—Thales, Anaximander, Anaximenes, and their successors, Xenophanes, Heraclitus, and Parmenides; the achievements in law and politics of Solon, Pericles, and Lycurgus; the dramas of Aeschylus, Sophocles,

Euripides, and Aristophanes; the sculpture and ar-
chitecture of Phidias; the histories of Herodotus and
Thucydides; and the philosophies of Socrates, Plato,
and Aristotle. Clearly, self-government under law,
which began before the age of Pericles and marked
the start of constitutional liberty in Western civilization, established a standard of Classical culture
which remained archetypal for many centuries in
Europe and America.

The free civil order of the *polis*, and the whole
dynamics of Greek society, were based upon a value
system inherent in Greek mythology. As Gilbert
Murray has shown in *Five Stages of Greek Religion*
(New York, 1925), the ancient Hellenic view of reality and their whole value system, which included
intellectual and civil freedom within their communal life, were provided for them by their religion.
Also, since the Greeks never set limits to the political
authority of the State, their religion, combined with
their strong family ties, created a buffer against arbitrary political power and made rule by law and custom superior to rule by wise men. As long as the
Greeks remained believers in their mythology and
their faith in the gods was ardent, their civilization
flourished, because they then possessed the
spiritual, moral, intellectual, aesthetic, and social
values and principles which produced a strong and
superior culture. Adherence to the ethical norms of
Greek mythology was essential to maintain the social
order of Hellas. Homer's *Odyssey* describes the
spiritual and political disorder brought into Greek
society by the vice of lust, through the eros of Paris
and Helen in bringing about the Trojan wars, and the

vice of pride in the wrath of Achilles in creating disunity among the Greeks. But beyond the symbolic myths of epic literature was the historical fact of the sophists, whose religious skepticism, moral relativism, and intellectual cynicism undermined the faith of the Greeks in their gods and shattered the basis of their civilization. Undoubtedly, the decline of the *polis* was facilitated by the atomized corporate structure of Hellenic society, by the strife between Athens and Sparta in the Peloponnesian War, and by the folly of Athenian politicians in the expedition against Syracuse; but the lack of courageous, prudent, and principled leadership during the age of Socrates and Plato resulted partly from the work of the sophists in destroying the spiritual foundations of Greek society.

Probably the most enduring contribution of ancient Greece to political liberty in Western civilization was in philosophy, particularly through Plato's *Republic* (however interpreted) and Aristotle's *Politics*. Like Socrates, they explored the nature of a just, well-ordered, and free society and perceived that the order in the *polis* rests on the order in the individual souls of men and citizens. These Greek philosophers believed that ultimately the spirit and character of man (the individual soul) and the nature of society (the body politic) were identical. Character largely determines national destiny.

Socrates first raised the crucial questions whether it is possible for a good citizen to be a wholly just man and, if so, whether it was possible for a just man to remain just and survive in a politically corrupt society. Socrates stood for the principles that it is better to suffer evil than to do evil; better to be punished for doing evil than to escape punishment; ultimately, that it is better to be martyred for justice than to murder for injustice. All of his principles were negated by the sophists. His trial, conviction, and execution proved that survival is not possible for a just man, because he will be either silenced through compromise, or exiled, or, as Socrates chose, executed. His fate showed that the moral salvation of a currupt society depends ultimately upon the willing martyrdom of its best men.

Socrates' execution had the same general symbolic significance for intellectual freedom and culture in ancient Greece that the crucifixion of Christ had for religion in the Roman Empire. The corrupt and pragmatically expedient political leaders of Athenian society, with their external respectability and inner moral depravity, find their counterpart in Pontius Pilate, who washed his hands of moral accountability and "truth" to release Barabbas and crucify Christ. (See *Matthew*, 27:21.) Meletus and Callicles were to Socrates, on the level of principle, as Judas Iscariot and Pontius Pilate together were to Christ, on the practical level. Socrates showed that the contrast between principled philosophers, the lawgivers of society, and unprincipled sophists, the false prophets who corrupt the souls of men, is a far better basis for judging human nature than social or economic class or race, religious creed, or nationality. Socrates' martyrdom established the principle that the moral disintegration of a society, modern as well as ancient, follows logically from the theories and methods of the sophists. But whereas in ancient times the end result of sophistry in politics was the martyrdom of Socrates and Christ, in our contemporary world the triumph of sophists and ideological politicians ultimately leads to the displacement of millions of innocent people or to their murder in concentration camps.

As Eric Voegelin has said, "On the level of pragmatic history, the philosopher is not the ordering force of society." (Voegelin, *Plato and Aristotle*, Baton Rouge, La., 1957, p. 301.) But on the level of enduring principles, in the realm of fundamental ethical laws, by which civilized men judge men and society, the flow of historical events on a purely empirical level has no moral significance or "reality." Plato posited the principle that the spiritual order in each soul and in society requires faith in a metaphysical order of "reality," a rational transcendent world of "Being" beyond "becoming," a realm of "Ideas" or "Forms," of "essences" beyond sensory appearances—in short, a world in which God ruled—from which emanated man's moral norms, by which Plato judged Athenian society and by which Western men have judged politics for centuries. Eric Voegelin has summarized Plato's achievement: "The Platonic vision of order has become part of reality, and while reality resists an embodiment of the Platonic idea it cannot escape the fate of being judged by it. The idea has become a standard." (Voegelin, *Plato and Aristotle*, p. 295.) The structure and normative order of society in historical time, as a process of revelation which includes meaning, can be perceived only by sound philosophy and religion. Science and the scientific method cannot provide such normative values and, indeed, are inimical to them. The enduring substance and meaning of history, its Logos or rational principle, springs from man's conscious relationship with God. Plato's metaphysical reality and valid normative principles and the Socratic method of discourse enabled him to triumph over the sophists. His principles became the philosophical language of Western civilization, providing the paradigm for political justice, order, and liberty.

Aristotle, a Macedonian Greek of Athenian descent, retained the Platonic dualistic metaphysics of spirit and matter but domesticated it to the world of the senses. He also perfected the intellectual tools of philosophy beyond that of any of his predecessors. He noted that "it is the mark of an educated man to look for precision in each class of things just so far as the nature of the subject admits" (Aristotle, *Nicomachean Ethics*, 1094, B, trans. David Ross, London, 1954, p. 3), a wise precept which our modern positivists, social scientists, and behavioralists would do well to heed. Like Plato, Aristotle perceived the soul as a one-man *polis*, whose need for self-government was the practical fulfillment of living in harmony with our total nature—the moral, intellectual, aesthetic, and social virtues. By insisting that Plato's aphorism, "Knowledge is virtue," is insufficient in practice and by making political virtue consist of knowledge combined wth virtuous action, Aristotle connected the uses of power in politics with the moral law. Beyond knowing good from evil, statesmen needed to have the moral courage to do what they knew was right. Aristotle's historical influence upon the medieval and early modern West is probably greater than that of any other philosopher. During the Middle Ages, his philosophy was combined with the Judaeo-Christian religious tradition to provide practical applications of religious principles to social and political matters. In every age to the present, Aristotle has affected the political thought of men who are concerned with the nature and function of government.

Although the Roman Republic (266 B.C. to 27 B.C.) and Empire (27 B.C. to 476 A.D.) were built upon brutal military conquests and sustained by slavery, nevertheless Rome contributed several vital elements to civil and political liberty in Western civilization. As Polybius noted, in less than fifty-three years, between 220-168 B.C., Rome conquered most of the lands around the Mediterranean Sea; and in the sixth book (fragment) of his *Histories,* he attributed the success in government of the Romans to their principle that power should be divided and balanced between the monarchical (executive) branch, the aristocratic senate, and the democratic assembly. Under the Republic, this structure in the State was essential in satisfying every segment of the citizen population, thus assuring good order, peace, justice, and freedom. Cicero held the same theory as Polybius. Montesquieu acknowledged that he derived his political principle of checks and balances from Polybius. Since the Founding Fathers of the American republic were educated in the ancient classics and studied Polybius and Cicero in school, and since some of them, including John Adams, Thomas Jefferson, and James Madison, had read

Montesquieu's *The Spirit of Laws,* their adoption of the principle that political power should be divided and balanced more likely came from Polybius, Cicero, and Montesquieu than from John Locke, who was himself indebted to the Roman classics. David W. Carrithers has summarized the influence of Monesquieu on these Founding Fathers:

"In 1760 a youthful John Adams noted in his diary that he had begun to read *The Spirit of Laws* and planned to compile comprehensive marginal notes to insure his proper attention to the work. Roughly a decade and a half later, Thomas Jefferson . . . devoted no less than twenty-eight pages of his *Commonplace Book* to extracts from this same work, and in 1792, in an essay on 'Spirit of Governments,' James Madison compared Montesquieu's role in the science of government to that of Francis Bacon in natural philosophy." (Preface, *The Spirit of Laws,* Berkeley, Cal., 1977, p. xiii. For a full account of Montesquieu's influence on these Americans and their contemporaries, see Paul M. Spurlin, *Montesquieu in America, 1760-1801,* New York, 1969, pp. 88, 153-157, 241.)

Under the Republic and extending into the early years of the Empire, the Romans established a *Pax Romana* which endured for over two hundred years (27 B.C. to 180 A.D.). Virgil's *Aeneid* testifies to the cultural life of Rome during the age of Augustus, when the arts of peace flourished as never before since the age of Pericles. At their best, the Romans combined the military virtues of Sparta with the sensuous and aesthetic traits in the humanistic culture of Athens. Although the Romans conquered the Greeks, it has become a commonplace that culturally the Greeks conquered the Romans. Long after Rome fell, far into the Middle Ages, the legend of its greatness provided a social, political, and cultural model for monarchs with ambitions to become emperors and for emperors who saw themselves as in the Roman tradition.

Between the late decades of the Republic and the early years of the Empire, the Greek political thought which had been absorbed into Roman politics began to develop toward monarchical absolutism. Emperors such as Augustus subordinated the senate and plebeian assembly to their power but claimed they were preserving the constitution of the republic and merely making central administration more efficient. In fact, the absolute rule of the *Principate* replaced the Republic with the Empire. Even under imperial power, good government was preserved by extending Roman citizenship beyond patricians to middle-class merchants, plebeians, foreigners, and even to freed slaves. Thus the Empire created a vast commonwealth of many races and religions, united under Roman law and language, and sustained by military force and civic virtues. Among the most esteemed civic virtues were *pietas*, *gravitas*, and *dignitas*. *Pietas* consisted of honor, loyalty, courage, fortitude, perseverance, self-discipline, self-sacrifice to civic duty, reverence to the gods, and magnanimity in victory. *Gravitas* was essentially a serious concern for the public welfare or social benevolence, and *dignitas* was the personal worth of an individual based upon honor, character, rank, or high office, which gave a noble style to Roman manners. These civic virtues, however much more admired than practiced, sustained the Republic and Empire through many crises.

Perhaps the greatest contributions to liberty of the Romans, beyond the theory and practice of divided political power, were the Stoic philosophy and the Justinian code of Roman laws. Roman Stoics from Cicero (106-43 B.C.) and Seneca (4 B.C.?-65 A.D.) to Marcus Aurelius (121-180 A.D.) set forth the theory of the moral natural law *(lex naturae),* which provided the moral basis for Roman jurisprudence, and culminated in the Justinian compilations of Roman laws (527-565 A.D.). The Justinian code established the inalienable right to life and private property and the principle that government is a rule of laws and not of arbitrary power by rulers. This meant that princes as well as citizens were subject to the rules of jurisprudence. These features of the Justinian code became the basis of the common law in many nations of Europe.

In 1757, Edmund Burke, in *An Essay Towards an Abridgment of the English History* (published in 1811), observed that Roman civil law combined with Christian morality and Teutonic tribal customs and manners to provide the foundations of European civilization. These elements were variously blended in different nations of Europe, but were infused in Church and State and even in the subordinate institutions of society to give Europeans their distinguishing character in the Christian commonwealth of Europe. For example, Roman law had a more profound and lasting influence in Scotland than in England, where the common law derived more directly from the canon law of the Church. After the fall of Rome, the Stoical moral natural law and Christian natural law theories became the basis of political philosophy in Europe, to at least the end of the eighteenth century. (For the vital place of natural law theory in the Middle Ages, see R. W. Carlyle and A. J. Carlyle, *A History of Medieval Political Theory in the West*, 6 Vols., New York and London, 1903-1936; for modern natural law in political theory, see Ernest Barker, *Natural Law and the Theory of Society: 1500-1800*, Ed. Otto Gierke, Cambridge, England, 1934. For a summary of the philosophical content and historical importance of natural law in shaping our concepts of good government, down to the late eighteenth century, see Peter J. Stanlis, *Edmund Burke and the Natural Law*, Ann Arbor, Mich., 1958, pp. 3-13.)

Medieval Constitutional Liberty and the Absolute State

It would require several volumes to do justice to the main historical events and philosophical principles of politics which helped to establish or destroy constitutional liberty in Europe from the Middle Ages to the founding of the American republic. The following summary merely describes some important developments, with emphasis upon England.

The eventual triumph of Christianity under Emperor Constantine (272-337) as the legally established religion of the Roman Empire was of immense importance in preserving the intellectual and cultural inheritance of Classical antiquity, including political philosphy. The contributions of Christianity to the intellectual foundations of liberty in Western civilization are not to be found in the hierarchical structure of the Church, which was centered in the absolutism of the Papacy. Since the lack of swift and efficient communication threw provinces upon their own resources in determining practical affairs on the diocese or parish level, papal absolutism was often ineffectual in regions remote from Rome. The religious contributions to liberty are rooted in the doctrines of Christianity which set a high moral value on individual souls and on the cultivation of the minds and creative powers in man.

Perhaps the most important intellectual and cultural achievement of the early Church fathers was the fusion of the Hebraic and Hellenic traditions, which in effect combined biblical revelation and philosophical reason, the moral virtues with the intellectual and aesthetic virtues. The bridge between the two great traditions had been built by Philo of Alexandria (c. 20 B.C.), a devout Jew and original thinker, who had applied Jewish law to his reading of Greek philosophy and united Moses with Plato, Aristotle, and other Greeks. (See E. R. Goodenough, *The Politics of Philo Judaeus*, New Haven, Conn., 1938. Of course, the high priests and leaders among orthodox Jews resisted being absorbed into a Graeco-Roman culture. After the fall of Jerusalem to the Babylonians, during the Diaspora, and again after the destruction of Jerusalem in 70 A.D., the Israelites were scattered and exiled from their homeland, and the great danger to their religion and freedom was that it would become diffused in doctrine, discipline, and ritual through compromise with other cultures. When Menelaus, a Jewish high priest, tried to unite Judaism and Hellenic philosophy, he was executed by the Maccabbees. Late in the Middle Ages, Moses Maimonides [1135-1204], who also discussed Jewish revelation in light of Greek philosophy in his *Guide of the Perplexed,* was looked upon with much skepticism by strictly orthodox Jews.) The harmony of the Judaeo-Christian conception of God and the metaphysics of Greek philosophy was established by St. Augustine (354-430), the greatest of the early Church fathers, when he read Plotinus' *Enneads* and interpreted this synthesis of Platonic philosophy in the light of the Christian doctrine of the Incarnation. (See Étienne Gilson, *God and Philosphy*, New Haven, Conn., 1941, p. 48 ff.) Medieval Christian theology and canon law developed from this fusion of the rational methods of Greek philosophy and biblical revelation.

From the time of St. Augustine's *De Civitate Dei*, with its distinction between the "City of God" and the "City of man," throughout the Middle Ages, Christ's words, "Render unto Caesar the things that are Caesar's and unto God the things that are God's," were interpreted to mean that Church and State were distinct and separate institutions, whose respective functions, the spiritual and temporal affairs of man, supplemented each other but required independent jurisdictions. Church and State frequently disagreed on where and how the lines of jurisdiction should be drawn. Churchmen claimed temporal powers, and kings claimed the power to appoint bishops. Also, social conditions in areas of Europe where the Teutonic barbarians had totally destroyed the State compelled the Church to assume the duties of the State, and these powers were retained beyond the emergency. But medieval political theory, best represented by St. Thomas Aquinas, sanctioned neither theocracy nor Caesarism. The two jurisdictions tended to balance each other, and a mixed and limited monarchical system was widely held to be the best constitution in the State, particularly in England and Germany. Passive obedience to an absolute arbitrary king was not an accepted doctrine.

Christianity taught that human life was sacred, a gift from God; that each individual soul was of equal value to God; that an informed conscience is the ultimate right in appeals to freedom; and that therefore man had God-given rights to life, liberty, and property which do not derive from the State and which the State has no moral or legal right to violate, even though it has the power. Although medieval society was highly stratified and social classes often lived quite apart, there was a profound sense of community that trancended classes, centered in a common religion. Medieval pluralism and diversity in nature and status functioned under the provincial feudal autonomy within the larger hierarchical orders in Church and State. Late in the Middle Ages, when the barons abused their feudal powers in raids upon weak neighbors, the Church instituted chivalry, a practical instrument to turn raw power against itself, to convert boors and barbarians on horseback into Christian knights who used their

military strength and skills to protect rather than to
pillage the weak, women, and children. The central
principle in chivalry was the same as in
government—to nullify "might makes right" by subordinating power to law and custom.

Beginning early in the sixth century, the Benedic-
tine monks at Monte Cassino abbey collected manu-
scripts of Classical antiquity, transcribed them in
their scriptorium, and funneled the learning of the
ancient world which had not been destroyed by wars
and fire to all the monastic religious orders though-
out Europe. It remained for the invention of printing
in Europe, by Johannes Gutenberg around 1440, to
complete the process begun by the monks and to
make the learning which they had preserved available to all educated Europeans.

Christopher Dawson has shown how the conversion of the pagan Roman world and the Teutonic
tribes to Christianity included their acceptance of a
harmonized Graeco-Roman, Judaeo-Christian culture. This constituted the most important and enduring basis in European civilization over the past
2,000 years. As Dawson put it, "Christian culture . . .
has created Western man and the Western way of
life." *(The Historic Reality of Christian Culture,*
New York, 1960, p. 17.) Dawson has described six
distinct stages in the development of Christian culture, each rich and diversified, from the primitive
and patristic Church to the present state of secularized Christianity. He notes that the close relationship which existed between religion and culture during the Middle Ages has been destroyed in
modern times, with consequences which are disastrous to contemporary man:

"Religion and culture are [not] two separate worlds with no relation to each other. The assumption of such a separation has been the great error of the Western mind during the last two centuries. First we have divided human life into two parts—the life of the individual and the life of the state—and have confined religion entirely to the former. This error is typical of bourgeois liberalism and nowhere has it been more prevalent than in the English-speaking countries. But now men have gone further and reunited the divided world under the reign of impersonal material forces, so that the individual counts for nothing and religion is viewed as an illusion of the individual craving for satisfaction. . . . This is the typical error of Marx and Engels and of the totalitarian mass state in all its forms." (Dawson, p. 17.)

Dawson's thesis, that religion creates culture and that culture provides the whole basis of civil society, including the legal and constitutional order of its political institutions, was assumed by Edmund Burke in his interpretation of the Middle Ages.

In his abridgment of English history, Burke noted that, after the Teutonic invaders had destroyed the Roman Empire in the West and "a great part of Europe" was in a most "deplorable condition," "the first openings of civility have been everywhere made by religion." (Burke, *An Essay Towards an Abridgment of the English History,* in *Edmund Burke: Selected Writings and Speeches*, Ed. Peter J. Stanlis, Garden City, N.Y., 1961, p. 66.) In England after the

Anglo-Saxon conquests, Burke observed, "Light scarce begins to dawn until the introduction of Christianity," which "soon made a sensible change" in the "rude and fierce manners" of the Saxons. (*Ibid.*, pp. 72-73.) In addition to Roman manners and laws, the monks introduced education because a knowledge of Scripture required learning. The development of these social and intellectual qualities through religion "in some measure removed all fear of the abuse of authority" and "induced the Germans to permit their chiefs to decide upon matters of . . . their private differences," which in time grew into the beginnings of the English constitution:

> "These chiefs were a sort of judges, but not legislators; nor do they appear to have had a share in the superior branches of the executive part of government—the business of peace and war, and everything of a public nature, being determined . . . by the whole body of the people, according to a maxim general among the Germans, that what concerned all ought to be handled by all. Thus were delineated the faint and incorrect outlines of our Constitution, which has since been so nobly fashioned and so highly finished. This fine system, says Montesquieu, was invented in the woods." (Burke, *Ibid.*, p. 75. For modern scholarly interpretations of the origins of the English constitution, see G. B. Adams, *The Origin of the English Constitution*, New York, 1912; A.F. Pollard, *The Evolution of Parliament*, London, 1920; and D. Pasquet, *The Origins of the House of Commons*, trans. by R.G.D. Laffan, London, 1964.)

Long before Burke, Samuel Daniel in his *A Defence
of Rhyme* (1602-1607) made the same point concerning the Teutonic origins of civil constitutions
throughout Europe: "The Goths, Vandals, and Lom-
bards, whose coming down like an inundation overwhelmed . . . all the glory of learning in Europe, have
yet left us still their laws and customs as the originals
of most of the provincial constitutions of Christen-
dom . . ." Burke noted that the social chaos of the
Middle Ages was greatly reduced by the development of Church and State: "In the midst of this chaos,
there were principles at work which reduced things
to a certain form, and gradually unfolded a system in
which the chief movers and main springs were the
Papal and the Imperial powers . . ." (*Ibid.*, p. 78.)
The distinct and largely separate powers of Church
and State were about equal in many parts of Europe,
and their rivalry, which required concessions on
both sides, "grew imperceptibly into freedom" and
"passed through the medium of faction and anarchy
into regular commonwealths." A series of charters by
kings to free cities, provinces, and religious orders
"laid the foundation of those successive charters
which at last completed the freedom of the subject."
(*Ibid.*, p. 79.)

English constitutional historians of the nineteenth
century considered Magna Carta (1215) the most
significant historical event for the progress of English constitutional liberty. The bill of rights which
Cardinal Langton drew up and which the barons of
England forced King John to sign limited by law the
power of the monarch over his subjects and denied
the theory that a king had absolute arbitrary

sovereignty through his prerogatives. In such vital matters as private property rights, the necessity of consent by the governed through their representatives in levying taxes, the right of *habeas corpus*, and the provision that no man could be punished but by the judgment of a court of law, the King's claim to absolute power was denied. As Burke said, Magna Carta "first disarmed the crown of its unlimited prerogatives, and laid the foundation of English liberty." *(Ibid.,* p. 83.) But Magna Carta was a medieval document and restored the feudal liberties and franchises which the barons had always claimed against the centralized authority of a national monarch, and was in no sense a step toward political democracy, as has sometimes been argued. Yet, as Burke noted, Magna Carta "went deeper than the feudal tenure, and affected the whole body of the civil government." *(Ibid.,* p. 83.) Gaillard Lapsley has noted the long-range effect of Magna Carta: "By the end of the Middle Ages the principles that taxes could not be raised nor legislation accomplished without the consent of parliament had long been accepted." (Gaillard Lapsley, preface to D. Pasquet, *The Origins of the House of Commons,* xiii.)

Until the Tudor period, the medieval constitutional system in England was that of a commonwealth in which all power in Church and State was perceived as emanating from God to mankind as a trust. In government, power was exercised through the representatives of the people in Parliament, with the King as a limited monarch at the head, and both branches were subject to natural law and to English common law. (See Sir James Fortescue, "De Natura

Legis Naturae," in *Works of Sir John Fortescue*, Ed.
Thomas Fortescue, London, 1869, Vol. I, p. 214 ff.)
George L. Mosse has described the legal and political philosophy of Sir John Fortescue (1394?-1476?)
as follows:

> "Fortescue's commonwealth was ... in the
> medieval tradition. There was here no theory of
> arbitrary might. The subject was endowed with
> certain concrete rights which no superior power
> could take away or change without his consent.
> ... These rights were enshrined in the laws and
> custom of the realm. But these laws and customs,
> and the rights which they protected, did not stand
> alone on their own merits. They were in turn
> protected by the superior law, the law of nature,
> which sanctified Fortescue's commonwealth,
> removed it from any merely human power. The
> people's rights and property were protected by
> this superior law because property had been a
> part of the law of nature long before nations were
> established. Indeed ... the secure enjoyment of
> this property was for him the essence of the
> founding of the commonwealth. Sanctity of pri
> vate rights and property was based on both the
> natural law and the original purpose of the state,
> and parliamentary statutes must be in conformity
> with the higher law." (George L. Mosse, *The
> Struggle for Sovereignty in England*, East Lan
> sing, Mich., 1950, p. 14.)

During the late Middle Ages, the English constitution sought to preserve the people's rights to life,
liberty, and property against *all* arbitrary power,

whether claimed by the King or Parliament. Neither
monarchical power nor popular power had any legal
claim to arbitrary or absolute rule, because the legal
sovereignty of both was strictly limited by moral
natural law and the common law of the realm. Before
noting how the medieval constitution was destroyed
in England under the Tudors, we might do well to
examine how it was undermined in theory on the
Continent.

The Classical and Judaeo-Christian political
philosophy, centered in the constitutional principle
that all rulers are subject to moral and legal restraints, received its most powerful attack from Nic-
colo Machiavelli (1469-1527), who has been called
the first modern political theorist. Lord Acton noted
that he rejected the moral tradition of Plato, Aristotle,
and the Stoics, as well as the Judaeo-Christian religious tradition: "For Machiavelli was nursed in the
pagan revival, and lived in a society notorious for
religious indifference, and for a refined immorality."
(F. E. Lally, *As Lord Acton Says*, p. 214.) Machiavelli
was keenly aware that he had made a complete break
with the Christian and Classical traditions.

In the introduction to the first book of his *Discourses on the First Ten Books of Livy*, begun before
writing *The Prince* (written in 1513 but not published until 1532), Machiavelli wrote: "I have re-
solved to open a new route, which has not yet been
followed by anyone." He repeated his claim of total
originality in political theory in Chapter 15 of *The
Prince*. The new route which Machiavelli provided,
deliberately opposed to "the general respect for antiquity" and its models for government based upon

moral norms, rested on his recognition that rulers
often do not act in accordance with the normative
principles they profess, but the reverse. Of course,
this banal fact of life had always been perfectly evident to every political theorist in the Classical and
Judaeo-Christian traditions. It did not require a
Machiavelli to inform the world that man's political
life was filled with horrendous crimes. But no writer
prior to Machiavelli had ever advocated that political
power should be pursued, as Acton put it, not merely
"by isolated acts of wickedness, but by a studied
philosophy of crime." (Acton, *History of Freedom*,
p. 41.) The chain of logic followed by Machiavelli
was that it was too difficult for men to live up to the
norms in Classical and religious political theory; that
those who attempted to live in accordance with such
norms were naive moral idealists; that in a world in
which knaves exercised power ruthlessly fools could
not survive; and finally that, given the empirical facts
of political power, the Classical and religious political philosophy should be rejected in favor of a new
political science which was realistic and recognized
no moral or legal limitations on rulers. Thus did
Machiavelli deify the Caesarian State, in which
political virtue included the shrewd use of vice.
Livy's history of the Roman Republic was chosen
because it ended before the Christian era began.
How the Roman rulers were able to conquer and rule
the ancient world provided Machiavelli with many
concrete examples of their actual behavior, which
was wholly indifferent to any ethical or legal considerations.

Machiavelli's *The Prince* set forth the total separation of "power politics" from metaphysics, religion, ethics, or law as controls and from any concern with the object of government in society. In his works, he advocates that rulers should assume the character of the lion and the fox; that they should maintain not virtue but the appearance of virtue; that if they thought it to their advantage in acquiring or sustaining power, they should not hesitate to engage in every form of expediency and subtle cunning, calculated intrigue, deceptive and treacherous diplomacy, clever opportunism, cruelty, terror, and force. These unethical acts, which modern admirers of Machiavelli have defended as "political realism" and even "inverted idealism," justified naked power both as an instrumental means and an end. Because the first law of politics was to get and hold power, it was justified for itself; the great object of power was to bring unity and order to society. Acton has summarized the modern conception of the State established by Machiavelli: "It was the supreme manifestation of the modern state according to the image which Machiavelli had set up, the state that suffers neither limit nor equality, and is bound by no duty to nations or to men, that thrives on destruction, and sanctifies whatever things contributed to increase of power." (Acton, *Lectures on Modern History*, pp. 50-51.) If *The Prince* is Machiavelli's recipe book for successful tyranny under an absolute monarchy, the *Discourses*, a much more subtle and complex work, makes the same case for absolute and unlimited republican government. The theory of political sovereignty, of the superiority of power to law, is the same in both works. One justifies the arbitrary will of a single tyrant; the other endorses the arbitrary will of a popular tyranny.

It is no accident and should surprise no one that Francis Bacon (1561-1626), who is widely hailed as the original lawgiver for modern empirical-rational science and who prided himself on harmonizing his mind with the true nature of material reality, accepted Machiavelli's central principle that politics should concern itself with what men do and not with what they ought to do. The resulting contrast between Plato's Classical and Bacon's modern view of politics is highly significant. Whereas Plato had said "Knowledge is virtue," Bacon, following Machiavelli's new science of politics and his own scientific method, said "Knowledge is power." Bacon's aphorism is the touchstone for all modern political science, as distinct from Classical and Christian political philosophy. In the eighteenth century, David Hume confirmed Bacon's aphorism and refined it into the principle that men cannot translate "is" into "should." Since indicative facts could not be converted into imperative norms, modern political science could not make moral judgments of rulers. Before Hume, Thomas Hobbes had claimed to found political science on geometrical reasoning. Modern positivism, value-free social science, and behavioralism in politics are the heirs of the Machiavelli-Bacon-Hobbes-Hume tradition. All of these writers, and many others who shared their values, have created an intellectual climate not only destructive of Classical and Judaeo-Christian political philosophy, but also of the means by which the American republic can be fully understood.

In the preface to L.A. Burd's great edition of *The Prince* (Oxford, 1891), Acton wrote: "The authentic interpreter of Machiavelli is the whole of later history." The contrast of what religious leaders said during the sixteenth century and what political rulers did made Acton remark that in that age "Calvin preached and Bellarmine lectured, but Machiavelli reigned." (Acton, "Freedom in Christianity," *Essays on Freedom and Power*, p. 71.) During this period in England, the Tudors gradually destroyed the medieval constitution and replaced it with the claim that the King had absolute sovereign power in all respects. Without ever having read Machiavelli, Henry VIII, through Thomas Cromwell, practiced the political precepts that the Italian thinker had set forth. (Although Tudor literature, particularly drama, contained about 400 direct references to Machiavelli, the image of Machiavelli was a myth, as the *Discourses* were not translated into English until 1636 and *The Prince* not until 1640. However, extracts from Machiavelli in French books which attacked his politics were available to English readers. Enemies of Cromwell accused him of being a disciple of Machiavelli.)

The most important initial step in the process of eliminating restraints on the King's power was the "Statute of Uses" passed by Henry VIII, which destroyed prescriptive legal rights to private property held for generations by transferring possession from the owners of land to those who used it. This statute permitted confiscation of the land of wealthy noblemen and the monastic orders. The enormous growth in absolute monarchical power through centralized national authority was at the expense of all the other competing corporate institutions—the feudal nobility, Parliament, free cities, guilds, the orders of the clergy, and commercial organizations. In England it was a happy accident that parliamentary government survived. In many parts of the Continent, the whole medieval representative system collapsed before the assault of monarchial power.

Tudor claims to arbitrary absolute monarchical power soon extended the royal prerogative beyond property rights to total control of the kingdom. Such writers as Sir Walter Raleigh, Sir Thomas Smith (Queen Elizabeth's Secretary of State), and Christopher St. Germain supported these claims. James I and Charles I tried to extend the royal prerogative by an appeal to "divine right," and in 1621 Parliament countered their claim with its own claim of a "divine right" of Parliaments. Sir Edward Coke, who failed in his attempt to uphold the medieval constitution, opposed the absolutist claims of James I, but he was imperfectly aware that the King's Parliamentary opponents held the same principle of sovereignty, but with a popular rather than a monarchial base. The conflict between the Stuart kings and the Puritan parliaments was not a struggle between monarchical tyranny and democratic constitutional government, as it has been portrayed, but rather between two rival claims to absolute arbitrary sovereign power, one monarchical, the other popular. Although both sides paid lip-service to law, neither side believed that its political power should be limited by natural law and English common law. Albertus Warren, an adherent of the parliamentary cause, frankly admitted that "the question never was whether we should be governed by arbitrary power, but in whose hands it should be." (Albertus Warren, *Eight Reasons Categorical, etc.*, London, 1653, p. 5.) Both King and Parliament held a common theory of sovereignty that defined law as the absolute power of whoever is the ruler. Thus whatever the ruler wills is law, without reference to moral natural law or common law. (See George L. Mosse, *The Struggle for Sovereignty in England*, East Lansing, Mich., 1950. Mosse's chapter "England's God on Earth," pp. 57-82, describes the King's claim to absolute arbitrary power, and his chapter "The Sovereignty of Parliament," pp. 83-106, describes the identical claims of Parliament.)

Thomas Hobbes set forth this conception of legal sovereignty most powerfully in *Leviathan* (1651), in defense of the King's party. But as it applied equally to Cromwell once the King was beheaded, Hobbes soon made his peace with his partisan enemies. Among the "classical republicans" of the seventeenth century, Andrew Marvell in his "Horatian Ode" to Cromwell (1651) praised Machiavelli as a good republican, as did James Harrington in *Oceana* (1656) and Algernon Sidney in *Discourses Concerning Government* (1682). To Hobbes as a monarchist and to Machiavelli and some of the Puritan republicans, the right of sovereignty was identical with absolute arbitrary power, unlimited by constitutional law. (Modern legal positivism holds the same view of sovereignty, the essence of which is that "might makes right." See John Austin, *The Province of Jurisprudence Determined*, London, 1861.) Acton, who held the opposite theory of political

sovereignty, that both King and Parliament are subject to moral and constitutional law, noted how
similar were such partisan enemies as Charles I and
Oliver Cromwell: "The divergence between any
two systems that result in arbitrary power cannot be
so great as that between either of them and a system
which subjects the sovereign to law." (Acton, review
of F. Arnold's *Public Life of Lord Macaulay*, in *Home
and Foreign Review*, January, 1863, p. 259.) Few
conflicts are more instructive for an understanding of
the American republic than the struggle for
sovereignty in seventeenth century England.

Constitutional Liberty and the American Republic

It should be self-evident from my preceding remarks that I believe the American republic, in its
total constitution, consists of much more than the
written federal Constitution. Perhaps no writer has
better understood the complex relationships between the American republic and all of Western
civilization than Orestes A. Brownson (1803-1876).
Woodrow Wilson considered Brownson's *The
American Republic: Its Constitution, Tendencies,
and Destiny* (1865), the best book on the American
constitution. (This book has been reprinted by Augustus M. Kelley, Clifton, N.J., 1972, and all references to Brownson's work will be to this edition).

Brownson was probably the first writer to distinguish between the written and unwritten American
constitution: "The constitution of the United States
is two-fold, written and unwritten, the constitution of
the people and the constitution of the government."
(*The American Republic*, p. 218.) The unwritten

constitution of the American people and society was shaped by its earliest and total historical and cultural inheritance from Europe and the eastern Mediterranean. The elements in Western civilization which most profoundly affected the American republic included the Judaeo-Christian religion and moral values; the Classical Graeco-Roman contributions to culture, law, and moral and political philosophy; the medieval concept of limited government; moral natural law and English common law; and the immediate English inheritance of seventeenth- and eighteenth-century colonists, particularly their colonial charters, but also their faith in science and human reason. The unwritten constitution consisted of what various people brought with them from Europe, from many nations, religions, and social and economic classes, as modified by the local or frontier conditions of life in America.

The unwritten constitution of Americans included their spirit, values, convictions, aspirations, and psychology, embodied in their growing sense of historical destiny, often based on a providential view of history. Brownson, like Abraham Lincoln and many nineteenth-century Americans, was imbued with the providential concept of history, which began very slowly to emerge after Columbus' discovery of the new world, as the whole course of empire took its way westward. The discovery and colonization of America proved to be a unique experience in the growth of liberty in Western civilization. In time the myth of America as "the promised land," "the new Eden," displaced the avaricious search for gold, or for a northwest passage to India and the spice islands. It was discovered that the greatest riches were in America itself, including freedom from the political and religious tyrannies of Europe. Both as a mythological reality and as historical fact and reality, America was not really "discovered" beyond geography until its colonies began to perceive that they belonged to the land as well as that the land belonged to them. They had to rid themselves of the idea that they were merely transplanted Europeans and to acquire a sense of being Americans. This process of self-identification entered into the psyche of Americans, both intellectually and politically, and gave shape to both the Declaration of Independence and the written Constitution. Culturally, the process of self-discovery as Americans was a theme often voiced by nineteenth-century American writers, including William Cullen Bryant, James Fenimore Cooper, Ralph Waldo Emerson, Herman Melville, Walt Whitman, and Mark Twain. America is hard to see because it is not easy to absorb the essence of Western civilization, and even in the twentieth century many Americans have yet to discover themselves in their two constitutions. The confusions about American society and culture, together with incredible misreadings of the provisions and amendments of the written Constitution, are among the most serious threats to the survival of liberty in the American republic.

The unwritten constitution of the American people and society, inherited from their colonial experience, preceded by over 180 years the formal framing and adoption of their written Constitution after securing independence from Britain. The customs, manners, spirit, convictions, culture, language, and character of the American people were already well-established and long functioning under their colonial and state charters before the federal Constitution became the basic law of the land. Since all the power in the federal Constitution derived originally from the people, corporately organized in the thirteen states, the written Constitution of the federal government was itself rooted in the unwritten constitution of the American people and society.

In discussing the unwritten and written constitutions it is necessary to distinguish sharply between the American Revolution and the written federal Constitution. Certainly the spirit of the Revolution entered deeply into the psyche of Americans. The slogan of the state of New Hampshire, "Live Free or Die," expresses well the vital part played by the American Revolution in our total historical experience, and its spirit forms a vital part of our unwritten constitution. The Revolution finds expression in the Articles of Confederation, and even in the written Constitution in the general fear of arbitrary centralized government. But while the Declaration of Independence was the first explicit claim that liberty is one of the great ends of good government, it does not prescribe any form of government, and the preamble of the Constitution identifies five other vital objectives prior to the desire to "secure the Blessings of Liberty to ourselves and our Posterity." The Declaration of Independence can indeed be read in the light of seventeenth- and eighteenth-century theories of the social contract, particularly the revocable contract of John Locke. But the federal

Constitution was not an attack on the abuses of power in government; it was a positive functioning model for a free republican government, the best, according to Alexis de Tocqueville, John Stuart Mill, and Lord Acton, that the world has ever known. (See for example Acton, *History of Freedom*, pp. 84-85. In the same year that Acton published his praise of the Constitution [1878], William Gladstone's essay, "Kin Beyond the Sea," described the American Constitution as "the most wonderful work ever struck off at a given time by the hand and purpose of man." *North American Review*, CCLXIV, 1878, p. 185.) Unfortunately, as Brownson noted, many interpreters of the American Constitution between 1787 and the Civil War fell into grievous errors by assuming Locke's social contract theory as the dominant element in discussing the American Constitution and society.

So much has been written on the moral and legal natural law philosophy of the Founding Fathers of the American republic that it is unnecessary to review that subject. (See for example Edward S. Corwin, *The "Higher Law" Background of American Constitutional Law*, Ithaca, N.Y., 1928, and Clarence E. Manion, "The Natural Law Philosophy of Founding Fathers," *University of Notre Dame Natural Law Institute Proceedings*, Vol. I, Notre Dame, Ind., 1949.) *The Federalist* papers of Hamilton, Jay, and Madison have also been so thoroughly analyzed that it is unnecessary to review this vast body of scholarship. But before considering the most important historical events and developments which have helped to weaken, destroy, or maintain constitutional liberty in the American republic, we may gain some historical perspective by examining a few observations of Hamilton and Madison.

These Founding Fathers of the republic took great pains in creating a "more perfect union" between the states and the federal government to avoid both the anarchy of the Articles of Confederation and the tyranny of majority will over minority rights which had plagued the ancient Greek and Roman democracies. They regarded the Articles of Confederation as the half-way house between the independence achieved by the Revolution and the liberty of full-fledged constitutional unity. As Hamilton noted in *The Federalist*, Number 9, the key to a democratic solution to the weaknesses of democratic government was found in the principle of divided and balanced powers:

> "The regular distribution of powers into distinct departments; the introduction of legislative balances and checks; the institution of courts composed of judges holding their offices during good behavior; the representation of the people in the legislature by deputies of their own election: these are means, and powerful means, by which the excellences of republican government may be retained and its imperfections lessened or avoided."

Hamilton was more aware than Madison of the danger that the republic might disintegrate, through "pure democracy" unchecked by law, so that he stressed whatever strengthened the federal authority. In *The Federalist*, Number 78, he justified judicial review as an essential process in constitutional government, even though it was not written into the federal Constitution. (The omission of the function of the Supreme Court in the written Constitution was probably not an oversight, as it has been depicted, but judicial review was so deeply rooted in the tradition of English common law and equity that when it was assumed by Chief Justice Marshall it was not opposed by Jefferson. Unlike King James I in confronting Coke's arguments, Jefferson recognized that legal equity differed from ordinary reason.)

Madison was more aware than Hamilton of the "encroaching nature" of political power as a weakness common to all mankind in all forms of government. (See *The Federalist*, Number 48.) In *The Federalist*, Number 10, Madison expressed confidence that the federal system was so well designed to control the power-hungry tendencies of legislators that centralized absolute power was impossible. He repeated this claim in *The Federalist*, Number 51. A strong pluralist society, with variety in unity rather than uniformity, was possible because "the rights of the minor party" were protected against even "an overwhelming majority." Thus was a "republican remedy for the diseases most incident to republican government" incorporated into the federal Constitution. In addition, Madison was convinced that the Constitution contained a principle which turned self-interest into public benevolence. It did this by "the policy of supplying, by opposite and rival interests, the defeats of better motives [which] might be traced through the whole system of human affairs, private as well as public." (*The Federalist*, Number 51.)

Both Hamilton and Madison were so convinced that the new federal Constitution would avoid both anarchy and tyranny that they predicted its adoption would prevent any possibility of a civil war between the states. (See *The Federalist*, Number 9.) During the Virginia ratifying convention, Patrick Henry had expressed the fear that the strong federal power, combined with its power to levy taxes, would endanger the public liberty of each state as a sovereign political body. Therefore, initially he favored rejecting the federal Constitution. Benjamin Franklin, in his essay "One Way to Wealth," had indicated in 1757 what he considered tyranny through taxation: "It would be thought a hard government that should tax its people one-tenth part of their time, to be employed in its service." Madison probably shared Franklin's view of tyranny in high taxes. He countered Patrick Henry's fear by arguing that the federal government was formed to protect the states from each other, not to tyrannize over them. The question was whether the Constitution provided a federal or a consolidated national government. Madison admitted it was "partly federal, partly national." But by preserving the people in their corporate character as citizens of their states and not uniting them in a uniform national state, the federal elements were strong enough "to exclude the evils of absolute consolidation, as well as a mere confederacy." Since the powers of the federal government are enumerated, Madison argued, the central government is limited in the objects of its concern, beyond which "it cannot extend its jurisdiction." On the power to levy taxes, Madison was even more confident that abuses of

federal power could not occur: "It can be of little
advantage to those in power to raise money in a
manner oppressive to the people." In direct reply to
Patrick Henry, Madison said: "But it is urged that its
consolidated nature, joined to the power of direct
taxation, will give it a tendency to destroy all subordinate authority; that its increasing influence will
speedily enable it to absorb state governments. I
cannot think this will be the case." Nothing is more
clear in historical retrospect than that the federal
Constitution failed to solve the problem of legal and
political sovereignty between the states and federal
government. (See Acton, "Political Causes of the
American Revolution," in *Essays on Freedom and
Power*, pp. 196-250. By the "American Revolution"
Acton means the rebellion of the South in the Civil
War.) Patrick Henry's second fear, that federal taxes
would become destructive of states and individuals,
was postponed until after the Sixteenth Amendment
was adopted in 1913: "The Congress shall have
power to lay and collect taxes in incomes, from whatever source derived, without apportionment among
the several States, and without regard to any census
or enumeration." Despite their many political
merits, as prophets of history Hamilton and Madison
left much to be desired.

The Federalist stands as proof that Publius wrote
mainly in hope and prophecy and that there is small
virtue in paper government as such. The long-range
history of the United States was to prove that both of
Patrick Henry's fears were justified. During the first
seven decades of the American republic, despite
great economic prosperity, the events of history were

to show that the principle of divided and balanced federal power, though sound as a safeguard against usurping absolute power, was inadequate to provide liberty on the state or local level. Constitutional liberty required that all the great interests in American society should be harmonized for individuals, institutions, and states. The written Constitution could not accomplish this without combining with the unwritten constitution of American Society and its people in the states and regions of the nation. By 1860, what Madison had denied could happen did happen in state-federal relations.

If Madison and Hamilton were primarily propagandists for the federal Constitution, the great explicators of its provisions and amendments were those who had to test it in practice, such as Chief Justice Marshall, John C. Calhoun, and Justice Joseph Story, and political philosophers with the advantage of historical hindsight, such as Orestes Brownson. Of these writers, in the period up to the Civil War, Calhoun (1782-1850) had perhaps the most profound understanding of the federal Constitution in relation to the unwritten constitution.

From around 1824 to his death in 1850, Calhoun rang the changes on his thesis that without an effective negative power to check centralized federal authority there was no constitutional liberty for individuals or states. The division of political power between the President, Congress, and Supreme Court was not in itself sufficient to assure liberty on the local or regional level. Both the legitimate interests of states as corporate bodies and of individuals in their many concerns were served better by the unwritten constitution than by the federal Constitution. The "Force Bill" of 1833, which enlarged the jurisdiction of federal courts, went far to nullify the political sovereignty of the states, without assuring more liberty to individuals. Calhoun developed his doctrine of "interposition," in which the state protected its citizens against the encroachments of federal authority by interposing itself between the federal government and its people. To make that protection legally effective, the logical extension of "interposition" was "nullification." These doctrines were centered in a strict construction of the provisions of the United States Constitution, which limited federal power, and were directed against the popular sovereignty doctrines of Jacksonian democracy.

Calhoun first applied his doctrines to partisan and regional differences over the protective tariff. This is important to note, because the common tendency to identify Calhoun's doctrine of "States' Rights" with the issue of slavery obscures the constitutional problem in a fog of emotionalism. Indeed, those who perceive the constitutional problem in terms of partisan or sectional disagreements over *any* public issue, rather than in terms of sovereignty and power in relation to federal-state rights and due process, will never understand the nature or importance of constitutional liberty in the American republic.

The retention of slavery under the federal Constitution was contrary to the very natural law principles on which the legal Constitution was based and to the spirit of religion in the unwritten constitution. The failure to eliminate it in the written Constitution proved disastrous to the peace and order of the American republic and almost led to its extinction. Calhoun's doctrine of nullification of federal authority by the states did not create a crisis over minor differences, but in a vital issue such as slavery, after all compromises were exhausted, it led logically to secession and civil war.

Calhoun's line of logical reasoning implied that the relationship of each state to the union was voluntaristic and based upon a social contract revocable at the corporate will of any state or group of states. No allowance was made for moral necessity out of the historical inheritance of the American people. On the principle of secession, no federal union, nor even any legal confederacy, could long exist. That Lockean theory was ultimately inconsistent with the very idea of unified corporate government. Ironically, the South fought to preserve slavery as an institution on the constitutional principle of political liberty for itself as a minority power defending minority rights against the majority will of the North, expressed through federal centralized power. The South saw itself as standing in relation to the northern dominated federal government as the thirteen American colonies had stood in relation to Britain. To the South, the Civil War was "the Southern war of independence." The defeat of the confederacy was not limited to the Southern states: all of the states, the victorious North as well as the defeated South, lost much of their constitutional sovereign power to the federal government.

The conflict over constitutional sovereignty and liberty clearly transcends the issues of tariff and slavery, because it applies to every concern of the American people in their response to federal and state authority. This fact is evident from the time of the adoption of the federal Constitution to the present. It is significant that the Republican Party, which had fought hard against "States' Rights" in the Civil War, upon becoming the decidedly minority party during Franklin D. Roosevelt's "New Deal," championed "States' Rights" against the federal programs they considered unconstitutional. Conversely, the Democratic Party, which had championed "States' Rights" and resisted the dominance of the Republican Party during most of the last four decades of the nineteenth century, upon acquiring power in 1932 became the great exponent of centralized national and federal authority. Nothing so illustrates Acton's precept that all power corrupts, and absolute power corrupts absolutely.

The Civil War was the great watershed in the political struggle over constitutional liberty in the American republic. The war settled the conflict over sovereignty between the states and federal power in favor of the federal government. The victory of the North preserved the Union, but what was preserved was not the union of federated states under the original written Constitution but a powerful centralized federal government in which external checks upon its authority were practically nonexistent. That this was in fact the case was not immediately clear, not even to such Americans as Brownson. During the Civil War, he praised the courage and wisdom of the American people in preventing the dissolution of the United States and assumed that the people would

restore the nation to its true constitutional principles. Brownson was well aware that the war effort of
the Union had centralized power in the federal government, particularly in the presidency. He also
noted that there was great danger that "the Union
victory will . . . be interpreted as a victory won in the
interest of social or humanitarian democracy" (*The
American Republic,* p. 365), a combination of Jacksonian mobocracy and Rousseauistic moral senti-
mentality fraught with great dangers to the future of
the American republic. The compulsory collectivist
and humanitarian social theory of Rousseau in the
Social Contract had not enjoyed much favor until the
abolition of slavery; after 1865 it grew in popularity.
As Brownson put it, Locke was displaced by Rousseau: "The tendency of the last century was to individualism; that of the present is to socialism." (*The
American Republic,* p. 71.) There was danger that
constitutional democracy would be overturned by
"the humanitarian democracy, which scorns all
geographical lines, effaces all individualities, and
professes to plant itself on humanity alone." (*The
American Republic,* p. 351.) But in 1861-1865
Brownson confidently asserted his faith in the traditional wisdom of the American people: "The great
body of the loyal people instinctively felt that pure
socialism is as incompatible with American democracy as pure individualism." (*The American Republic,* p. 356.) After the Union victory, during the last
decade of his life, Brownson suffered a profound
disillusionment in the American people and their
leadership.

The decade of southern Reconstruction under

Presidents Johnson and Grant was to Brownson an
utter disaster to the American republic. He favored a
policy of reconstruction based upon his principle of
territorial democracy. Brownson held that the southern secession was an illegal territorial or corporate
rebellion of states, "an organic, organized political
rebellion," not merely against federal authority but
against the constitutional union. Constitutional
sovereignty resided not in the federal government
alone, nor in any individual or group of states, but
only in all the states united. Therefore, the southern
leaders and population could not legally take their
territorial states out of the union, because the American republic was in the states united and not in any
section of the people at large. This was Brownson's
legal basis for rejecting states' sovereignty apart from
the federal Constitution, while retaining states'
rights under the Constitution. By seceding, the
southern states lost none of their natural and civil
rights as territorial and organic societies, but all of
their political rights as members of the Union. On
these grounds, Brownson advocated a policy of reconstruction based upon magnanimity, to restore the
Union whole by following the constitutional
methods of the past in admitting new states into the
Union. This meant that upon the defeat of the South
the existing state governments could petition to be
readmitted into the Union, and the federal government could recognize each elected state government
as representing the corporate people of that state. As
Hugh Marshall has noted, if Brownson had lived
beyond 1876, "he would have seen very shortly that
his proposed reconstruction program had indeed

been judged the only workable one for the nation during that period." (Hugh Marshall, *Orestes Brownson and the American Republic,* Washington, D.C., 1971, p. 274.)

Unfortunately for the nation and for Brownson's faith in the American republic, the federal government, totally dominated by the radical abolitionist wing of the Republican Party, adopted a vindictive reconstruction policy, which treated the South as conquered territory to be exploited and the southern people as outlaws and criminals. Brownson vigorously condemned the attempt of such leaders as Senator Stevens and Representative Bingham to consolidate all the powers and rights of individuals and states into the federal government in Washington, D.C., which they controlled. In particular, Brownson criticized the Fourteenth Amendment (1868) and the Fifteenth Amendment (1870), which under the guise of expanding the scope of "due process," "equal protection under the law," and "privileges and immunities," actually gave control of suffrage to the federal government, thus expanding the scope of federal authority at the expense of the states. Brownson perceived that the real object of these amendments was not to extend freedom to all Americans but to consolidate the political power of the Republican Party through control over the emancipated slaves and a prostrate disenfranchised white South.

Although the Fourteenth and Fifteenth Amendments to the federal Constitution were passed according to legal requirements, nevertheless they were revolutionary innovations by the Republican

Party, because they tended to destroy the United
States under federalism in favor of uniformity in
population under consolidated nationalism.
Brownson summarized their revolutionary nature:

> "They are revolutionary in their character and
> tendency, and destructive of the providential or
> unwritten constitution of the American people,
> according to which, though one people, they are
> organized as a union, not of individuals, but of
> states, or political societies, each with an au-
> tonomy of its own. . . . The Union leaves to each
> state its individuality, and any proposed amend-
> ment that would merge the individuality of the
> state in that of the Union, would be unconstitu-
> tional, for it would tend to destroy both the state
> and the Union. . . . Give to congress or the Union
> the power to determine who shall or shall not be
> the political people of a state, and the state no
> longer exists; you merge the state in the Union,
> obliterate state lines, and convert the republic
> from a federal into a centralized or consolidated
> republic, or a pure democarcy in which the con-
> stitutions count for nothing, and the majority for
> the time have unlimited power." (Orestes
> Brownson, *Works*, XVIII, pp. 254-55.)

Brownson's essential thesis has been confirmed by a
wealth of evidence in Raoul Berger's *Government
by Judiciary: The Transformation of the Fourteenth
Amendment* (Cambridge, Mass., 1977.) On March
12, 1866, Brownson noted that the unconstitutional
process to secure unlimited power on a national
scale, based upon numbers, began as soon as the

Civil War was over: "The leading Radicals in Congress tend to consolidation, and would, if successful, destroy the distinctive excellence of the American System, entirely eliminate the federation element, and make the government a centralized democracy, the worst of all possible governments." (Brownson Papers, Archives of the University of Notre Dame, III, 3-a, March 12, 1866.)

The extinction of slavery as an institution was to the Republican Party leadership an opportunity to enslave the entire nation to its political power. Brownson opposed their plan for a consolidated national government based upon popular sovereignty, because it would lead to political and legal despotism.

The consolidation of legal and political power in Washington, D.C., injured all the states, northern as well as southern. In January 1874, Brownson noted that the Republican Party was "not only fearfully corrupt, but . . . manifestly consolidationists, and therefore disloyal to the American constitution." (Brownson, *Works*, CVIII, p. 546.) During the vital years 1866-1876, Brownson concluded that the Republican Party was "the most unconstitutional, unscrupulous, un-American, and dangerous party that has ever arisen in the country . . . a party that scoffs at constitutional restraints, and acts on the principle that might is the only measure of right, and that the party that can command a majority of votes may do whatever it pleases." (Brownson, *Works*, XVIII, p. 251.) In his final years, Brownson was bitterly disillusioned that the American people were willing to support the avarice, corruption, and unconstitutional

tyranny of the Republican Party. Yet a year after
Brownson's death in 1876, with the inauguration of
Rutherford B. Hayes in March 1877, following a
political deal between Hayes and southern electors,
a new policy of reconstruction based upon
Brownson's principle of territorial democracy was
begun. Although the earlier principles of constitutional freedom were weakened in favor of equality of
condition, the American republic was restored to its
original constitutional principles.

If Brownson's description and interpretation of the
American republic is taken as an archetypal statement or norm of what the federal-state system was at
its original best and what it should be throughout its
historical development, then one vital question remains: Has the American republic maintained its
basic structure, principles, and spirit since
Brownson's death over a century ago?

It does not require a deep or extensive knowledge
and understanding of American history during the
past century to show that every war, every economic
depression, and every national and even international crisis has resulted in a growth in power of the
federal government and eventually in a corre-
sponding serious erosion in the power of state and
local governments. The territorial democracy of the
states, which preserved the sense of regional and
local freedom in community life up to 1860, has been
weakened steadily in favor of a leveling consolidated
federal government. Until 1860, territorial democracy and constitutional federalism together had asserted states' rights without disintegration and federal union without consolidation. This relationship

and process involved separation of two kinds of coordinated political powers—state and federal—rather than merely a system of conflicting checks and balances within the federal government. Until 1860, the American people had developed from colonialism to independence to confederation to federal constitutional nationhood. After 1865 American society became badly unbalanced in both its unwritten constitution and the written federal Constitution, with the religious spirit yielding to the secular and material, the rural to the industrialized urban and metropolitan, the states to the federal government, the Congress to the presidency, and everything in and out of government to an entrenched, growing, avaricious, self-seeking bureaucracy.

From the perspective of the twentieth century, Brownson showed remarkable insight in perceiving that after 1865 the more consolidated federal government would appeal to the "general welfare" clause of the Constitution in order to justify its growth in power. He noted that this increase in federal power would also be at the expense of both the political power of the states and the personal freedom of each citizen, because the private welfare of each was identified and merged with an assumed "general welfare" on the national level, and would thus deny the constitutional principle of a division of powers between federal and non-federal regional, state, and private interests:

"The private welfare of each is, no doubt, for the welfare of all, but not therefore is it the 'general welfare,' for what is private, particular in its nature, is not and cannot be general. To understand by general welfare that which is for the individual welfare of the greater number, would be to claim for the General government all the powers of government, and to deny that very division of powers which is the crowning merit of the American system." (Brownson, *The American Republic,* pp. 261-262.)

Thus the "general welfare" clause was used to reinforce the consolidation of federal power already achieved by the Fourteenth Amendment to the Constitution. It further expanded federal power at the expense of the states by making citizenship more national than territorial and by subordinating the jurisdiction of the states over its citizens to federal jurisdiction.

Another of Brownson's remarkable insights and approaches was his warning that with the Union victory the greatest danger to constitutional liberty in the American republic was in the development of a humanitarian and egalitarian democratic socialism. He observed that this form of so-called "pure democracy" rested not upon natural law or constitutional law, but upon an abstract ideological concept called "humanity," and assumed that society consisted of isolated masses of individuals told by the head, with no corporate character. In pursuit of its ends, democratic socialism set aside the natural and civil rights of individuals and of individual states and recognized no territorial limits to its growth and power. When combined with appeals to the "general welfare," humanitarian and egalitarian democratic socialism was thoroughly destructive of individual rights and of the state-federal constitutional system of the American republic.

According to Brownson, the essence of democratic socialism was the doctrine that the economic and social good of men lies exclusively in the natural order, and that such goals are not attainable by individual free efforts but require constant intervention and support by the federal government in a controlled society. Democratic socialism assumed that all human problems, but especially economic ones, require a public solution through politics, and thereby it greatly weakened individual freedom and self-reliant responsibility by subordinating everyone to its social collective actions. Thus democratic socialism was at once thoroughly materialistic and politically collectivist, the very reverse of the Judaeo-Christian religious tradition and constitutional liberty through divided powers. The spiritual nature of individually free men had little place in democratic socialism. Despite the contradictions between them, Brownson perceived that democratic socialism would win many converts among Jews and Christians by veiling itself under the religious language of love and charity and by claiming that through the social benevolence of the state, humanity would be emancipated from poverty and other evils.

Historically, the practical instrumental means by which democratic socialism implemented its economic and social theories and programs, at the expense of the territorial democracy of the states, was the passage of the Sixteenth Amendment to the

Constitution, the federal income tax (1913). The congress which passed this amendment was anything but socialistic. Before examining the effects of the federal income tax upon American constitutional democracy, it will pay us to note the gap between what legislators intend and what often results from their work. The sponsors of the Sixteenth Amendment expressed their conviction that the federal income tax on Americans would never exceed 2 percent—a prophecy which stands on a par with the delusions of Hamilton and Madison that adoption of the federal Constitution would prevent any civil war and would never result in the growth of federal power at the expense of the states. Indeed, the history of the losses in constitutional liberty for states, institutions, and individuals could be written in terms of the unforeseen consequences of interpretations by the Supreme Court of provisions and amendments to the federal Constitution which are wholly at variance with the intentions of the framers of the Constitution and those who have amended it.

For example, the First Amendment, forbidding "an establishment of religion, or prohibiting the free exercise thereof," was clearly intended to free government from legal ties with any particular religion and to make all religions free from government control, so that each could flourish and fulfill its social function. The amendment was intended to guarantee religious freedom in the private and public life of America, while keeping Church and State legally separated. It has been interpreted to mean that religion should have no place in the public life of the nation, thus creating an unofficial kind of atheism or secularism by establishment, under which no religions have any social rights. The First Amendment, added to protect religious freedom, has been converted into a weapon against religion. Similarly, the Fourteenth Amendment has also departed radically from the designs of the Republican politicians of the Thirty-ninth Congress (1868). This amendment took from the states essential powers regarding the franchise, citizenship, and legal rights regarding sexual and racial relationships. Also, following a revolutionary innovation begun with the Thirteenth Amendment in 1865, the Fourteenth Amendment shifted the enforcement of its provisions from the judiciary to Congress. Thus was due process further weakened as the essential method in adjudicating constitutional conflicts and replaced with government by federal fiat through powers delegated by Congress to federal agencies and departments.

The unforeseen consequences of legal interpretations of the Constitution radically at variance with the intentions or purposes of its sponsors has further weakened constitutional restraints upon federal power. Much has been written during the twentieth century about judges who substitute their private reason, will, or social or economic theory for the original meaning of a law or constitutional provision. The lack of judicial restraint reached heights of abuse beyond anything known in the nineteenth century, as legal positivism came more and more to prevail in the twentieth century. As Alexander M. Bickel has proved, the Supreme Court under Justice Earl Warren was radically expedient in interpreting the law during the 1950s and 1960s to shape legislation to what it considered desired social results. (See Alexander M. Bickel, *The Supreme Court and the Idea of Progress,* New York, 1970.) Instead of preserving the constitutional separation and limitation of politicial power through judicial review with reference to prescriptive legal norms and due process, since the 1950s the Supreme Court has often become the means of destroying constitutional restraints upon legislative, executive, and bureaucratic power.

For two decades after the income tax amendment was passed, it lay dormant and had no practical or theoretical effect on federal-state relations. But it became sharply activated during Franklin D. Roosevelt's "New Deal" in its attempts to solve the problems of the Great Depression. During the 1930s gradual increases in the rates of the income tax, combined with appeals to the "general welfare" and interstate commerce clauses of the federal Constitution and executive and legislative hostility against due process through judicial review, resulted in legislation which nullified many former constitutional restraints upon the federal government. The great majorities enjoyed in both houses of Congress by the Democratic Party revived the assumptions underlying popular sovereignty—that majority will supercedes constitutional law in American democracy. Also, for the first time in the history of the American republic, the federal government entered into very extensive "make work" programs in conservation, education, the arts, public health, public works, etc., as part of its antidepression social welfare program. When the Supreme Court declared legislation for these programs unconstitutional,

Roosevelt attempted to pack the Court with judges sympathetic with his economic objectives. When this failed, he appointed judges who conceived of judicial review as an instrument of social justice, in accordance with humanitarian and egalitarian social and economic theory, rather than with constitutional norms and due process. Since Roosevelt extended his political power into four terms, such appointments to the Supreme Court dominated the courts for an entire generation.

During the "New Deal," the Keynesian theory of economics was adopted. (See John Maynard Keynes, *A Treatise on Money*, New York, 1930; *Unemployment as a World-Problem*, Chicago, 1931; *The General Theory of Employment, Interest, and Money*, New York, 1965. See also Lawrence R. Klein, *The Keynesian Revolution*, New York, 1961; William H. Hutt, *Keynesianism–Retrospect and Prospect: A Critical Restatement of Basic Economic Principles*, Chicago, 1963; Sidney Weintraub, *A Keynesian Theory of Employment, Growth and Income Distribution*, Philadelphia, 1966.) Through this theory, the federal government was made supreme in the regulation and control of industry, business, banking, agriculture, and other interests, under a revolutionary policy of taxation of both personal and corporate incomes. Instead of levying taxes to meet the necessary expenses of government within a balanced budget, the federal government created new economic and social welfare programs on a gigantic scale—affecting every area of American life, including some expressly prohibited by the Constitution—in order to justify greater and greater graduated income taxes. The federal government spent more and more of the gross national product under a system of credits and almost unlimited deficit spending. The grand object of the "New Deal" was egalitarian "distributive justice," which was based on the assumption that all men, whether or not they are able or, indeed, willing to work, have an equal right to the benefits of the nation's common temporal goods and services. In politics this view meant pitting classes against each other, exploiting the envy of the poor against the rich, to gain or keep political power. In society it meant that even in times of great prosperity, long after the Great Depression, millions of Americans were made content to depend upon the federal government for all or part of their support. The end result was the creation of the welfare state with an enormously expanded federal bureaucracy to serve its programs and needs. In theory and in the public propaganda of government and press, the bureaucracy exists in order to serve the welfare state. In practice, the reverse is also true: The welfare state is perpetuated and expanded in order to justify and serve the private interests of the bureaucracy. In the process of serving the Leviathan state, the bureaucracy takes very good care of itself, through civil service job security, amounting to perpetual tenure, and through extremely generous retirement benefits.

Historically, the intellectual foundations of the modern welfare state rest upon two important developments: a faith in science and the scientific method applied to human affairs and an unquestioned belief in the natural moral goodness of man.

These two beliefs have combined to create an almost unbounded confidence in many Americans that paternalistic government in the form of a popular, secular, and benevolent Caesarian state can perform god-like miracles in solving the problems of poverty, crime, ignorance, war, disease, etc. It would take a small volume to trace how from the seventeenth-century science of Bacon, Descartes, and Hobbes and from eighteenth-century Rousseauistic "sensibility," these articles of faith have come to be assumed by many contemporary Americans. (For a brief account of how the scientific method entered and developed in politics and a critical rebuttal of it, see Peter J. Stanlis, "Edmund Burke and the Scientific Rationalism of the Enlightenment," in *Edmund Burke, the Enlightenment and the Modern World,* Detroit, 1967. Sir Isaiah Berlin has also shown that the application of the scientific method to human affairs is the central object of the Enlightenment. See his "Introduction," *The Age of Enlightenment,* New York, 1956. Ernst Cassirer has argued for the empirical more than the rational basis of the scientific method in *The Philosophy of the Enlightenment,* Boston, 1955.) The belief that through science man can bring not only physical nature but also historical destiny under rational control underlies the idea of progress as a law of history, which is also part of the intellectual machinery of the welfare state. The emotional dimensions for the modern social consciousness flow from a sentimental conception of human nature, which assumes that man is innately good, that all evils or failures result from external social conditions, that a benevolent and all-powerful State can remove inequality through behavioral modifications and expropriation of wealth. (For the genesis and historical development of "sensibility" and the belief in the natural moral goodness of man as the basis for the modern welfare state, see Peter J. Stanlis, "The Modern Social Consciousness," *The Occasional Review*, Vol. 1, No. 1, February 1974.)

Reinhold Niebuhr has remarked on a certain similarity between contemporary American and Soviet Russia regarding their view of science and of progress in history:

> "There is great irony in the fact that mankind is at the moment in the toils of the terrible fate of a division between two great centers of power, one of which is informed by the communist and the other by the bourgeois liberal creed of world redemption. Both creeds imagine that man can become the master of historical destiny. The communists assume that the rationalization of particular interest will disappear with a revolutionary destruction of a society which maintains special interest. The very fury of communist self-righteousness, particularly the identification of ideal ends with the tortuous policies of a particular nation and its despotic oligarchy, is rooted in its naive assumption that the rationalization of partial and particular interests is merely the product of a particular form of social organization and would be overcome by its destruction. . . . Meanwhile the liberal world dreams of the mastery of historical destiny by the gradual extension of the 'scientific method' without recognizing that the

objectivity and disinterestedness which it seeks by such simple terms represents the ultimate problem and despair of human existence." (Reinhold Niebuhr, *Faith and History*, New York, 1949, pp. 83-84.)

The idea that science, sentiment, and history will redeem mankind from all its griefs and grievances has no place in a conception of the American republic in which political power is controlled and limited by constitutional law. Implicit in the traditional view of American society is the belief that human nature, with all its positive capability for self-rule, is morally flawed and needs to protect itself from absolute power.

Lord Acton has well summarized the vital distinction between the true democratic principles of constitutional republican government, which limit power in rulers in order to preserve freedom, and the false principles of democratic socialism, which pervert constitutional government by demanding unlimited power for a supposed majority will:

"The true democratic principle, that none shall have power over the people, is taken to mean that none shall be able to restrain or to elude its power. The true democratic principle, that the people shall not be made to do what it does not like, is taken to mean that it shall never be required to tolerate what it does not like. The true democratic principle, that every man's free will shall be as unfettered as possible, is taken to mean that the free will of the collective people shall be fettered in nothing." (Lord Acton, "Sir

Erskine May's 'Democracy in Europe,' " in *Essays on Freedom and Power*, p. 159.)

These two conceptions of democracy—constitutional representative republicanism and democratic socialism—are totally antithetical to each other regarding liberty in the American republic. (For an analysis of their differences in many matters other than liberty, see Raymond English, *Constitutional Democracy vs. Utopian Democracy*, Washington, D.C., 1983; and Claes G. Ryn, *Democracy and the Ethical Life*, Baton Rouge, La., 1978.) Democratic socialism bases its claims upon an absolute popular will and recognizes no constitutional limitation on its political power. Edmund Burke's aphorism that the tyranny of a multitude is a multiple tyranny applies well to democratic socialism.

To the extent that the American federal government has deprived the state-federal system of independent power and initiative, constitutional democracy has been replaced by democratic socialism. Of course, the formal state-federal structure still exists, but as an effective safeguard against federal power the states are largely moribund. Nor is there sufficient balance in the divisions of power within the federal government to protect the freedom of Americans in their heterogeneous social and economic interests or to harmonize them into a healthy community life. National politicians of both parties, but particularly the socialist wing of the Democratic Party, pay scant attention to constitutional restraints upon federal programs which they justify by popular opinion polls. Once passed, their legislation is often given over to be administered by various departments of bureaus, from whose arbitrary decisions individuals and states cannot easily escape. The federal government has become almost all in all, and individual citizens and states have adjusted themselves to its overwhelming power. The national government, through its extensive propaganda apparatus and backed by the press, radio, and television news, always stresses the humanitarian nature of its programs and begs the question of their compatibility with the intentions of our Founding Fathers. But the egalitarian benevolence of federal programs is invariably compulsory, so that the area of individual freedom becomes more and more restricted as federal benefits are accepted. As citizens become more dependent on the federal government, the American republic becomes more and more politicized, secularized, collectivized, and bureaucratized.

The conflict between personal liberty and Caesarism in the State is perennial throughout history. In rulers the lust for power over others always threatens mankind, and in every generation opportunistic and unprincipled men are found ready and eager to ally themselves with tyrants, even benevolent tyrants, to keep their fellow citizens in subjection. Among rank-and-file Americans in the twentieth century, far too many are content to sacrifice their constitutional liberty for promises by politicians of economic security. Liberty has never been a free gift of any absolute state, and there is no security in tyranny. Although many men in public life pay lip service to freedom, always the genuine love of liberty, and even the understanding of liberty, is rare.

Yet liberty is such a vital source of energy in individuals and in society and the State itself that without it a society invariably decays. The more the
safeguards of the written federal Constitution are
eroded or destroyed, the more we need to depend
upon the unwritten constitution which derives from
the moral character and values of the American
people.

American politics has always been torn by internal
conflicts. Many of these differences are merely the
clashes of partisan and personality rivalries. The
more deeply rooted conflicts are philosophical and
stem in part from ambiguities and contradictions in
both the written and unwritten constitutions in the
American republic and from the myths and
ideologies of our revolutionary era. The great choice
before the American people is between constitutional liberty and bureaucratically imposed
socialism in which individual freedom ranks low in
the scale of values. To restore and preserve individual liberty in a just and constitutionally ordered
society is the great domestic task remaining before
us in the future decades. We need to remind ourselves that man is not God, and also that men do not
live by bread alone. The threat of annihilation
through nuclear war has at least put an end to the
fatuous optimism that science and history will redeem mankind. Communism and all ideologies
which claim to have control over historical destiny
are an external threat to our survival. But if Americans as a nation live out the historical destiny of the
republic, they will yet restore their battered constitution and preserve their liberty. Many Americans

still move to the measure of the principles of constitutional liberty laid down by the Founding Fathers. It should take but a few great and resolute leaders, with courage and understanding, to restore to the mass of our people a sense of how much liberty has been lost and the need to restore it.

Professor Leo Strauss once observed that "The United States of America may be said to be the only country in the world which was founded in explicit opposition to Machiavellian principles." (*The Prince*, New York, 1977, p. 183.) This statement is paticularly valid as applied to the conception of the moral nature of man in relation to constitutional liberty. The Founding Fathers of the American republic were mainly orthodox Christians, and as such avoided both the naiveté of the Rousseauistic theory that man is by nature innately good and the converse Machiavellian cynicism that man is by nature depraved beyond spiritual redemption. Thus they believed that man has enough goodness in him to rule himself according to the principles of constitutional democratic liberty, but that no man or set of men were good enough to be given absolute power. The Founding Fathers understood Acton's aphorism that all power tends to corrupt and that absolute power corrupts absolutely. The American republic, in both its written and unwritten constitution, was based upon a realistic conception of man's moral, intellectual, and social nature. The first step in the process of restoring our lost liberties may well be to recapture their realistic conception of man.

WORLD PERSPECTIVES
IN INTERNATIONAL LAW:
MORAL VALUES IN RELATIONS
ACROSS NATIONAL BOUNDARIES

by

Richard Young

Richard Young

Mr. Young earned his B.A. at St. Lawrence University in 1940 and his J.D. at Harvard University in 1947. He was admitted to the New York Bar in 1947 and was associated with Manley O. Hudson, Professor of International Law at the Harvard Law School and former Judge of the Permanent Court of International Justice, in his private practice from 1948 to 1956.

In 1956, Mr. Young took up the private practice of international law in Van Hornesville, New York. His special fields of interest are the law of the sea, development of ocean resources, protection of private investment abroad, and international arbitration and procedures for dispute settlement.

Mr. Young served as a consultant to the U.S. Naval War College from 1965 to 1970 and as an Adjunct Professor of Law at Syracuse University College of Law in 1976-1977. He has lectured at the annual Academy of American and International Law of The Southwestern Legal Foundation since 1964.

The author of many professional papers and contributions to legal journals and a member of a number of professional societies, Mr. Young served as a member of the State Department Advisory Committee on the Law of the Sea and as an adviser to the Third United Nations Conference on the Law of the Sea from 1970 to 1982. He has been a member of the Advisory Board of the International and Comparative Law Center of The Southwestern Legal Foundation since 1964, and served as its Chairman from 1966 to 1968. He was a member of the Executive Board of the Law of the Sea Institute from 1971 to 1980 and served as its Presiding Officer from 1977 to 1980.

Mr. Young is Vice Chairman of the Board of Trustees of St. Lawrence University and Director of the State Bank of Albany in Albany, New York. He serves as Vice Chairman of the Herkimer County Planning Board and Secretary and Treasurer of the Van Hornesville Community Corporation, and was President of the Central New York Heart Association in 1971-1972.

WORLD PERSPECTIVES
IN INTERNATIONAL LAW:
MORAL VALUES IN RELATIONS
ACROSS NATIONAL BOUNDARIES

by Richard Young

"No man is an island, entire of itself," wrote John Donne three and a half centuries ago. "Every man is a piece of the continent, a part of the main." The great English preacher was speaking in a moral sense of the deep truth that every human being is not only an individual but also a member of the human community. So, he went on in a famous passage, "any man's death diminishes me, because I am involved in mankind; and therefore never send to know for whom the bell tolls; it tolls for thee."

"Because I am involved in mankind." The message is more pressing today than when it was written. In Donne's time—though no one knows for sure— there were probably no more than half a billion people in the whole wide world. Today there are some nine times that, and the figures are still going up. But that is not all. Not only are there vastly more people; modern science and technology have linked them more closely together than ever before, and at the same time have brought about a degree of economic interdependence never known in past history. This interdependence is self-evident and needs no belaboring here. When oil supplies from the Middle East are threatened, when financial crisis looms in Argentina or Brazil, when violence breaks out in Lebanon or Chad, we all feel the shock waves, and we are all "diminished" accordingly. "Send not to know for whom the bell tolls"; it tolls for all of us, involved as we are, more than ever before, in mankind.

Besides growth in population and growth in interdependence, there has been a tremendous increase in recent years in the number of political units, chiefly national states, which are participants in the global community. the great colonial empires—Britain, France, Portugal, Spain—are gone, except for the Soviet Union, and political colonialism is a thing of the past. Most of their many fragments stand now as states in their own right. The numbers tell the story. In 1945 fifty-one states signed the United Nations Charter, out of perhaps some sixty-five states in the world. Today the membership of the United Nations has more than tripled, to 157 at my last count, with perhaps a dozen more states which are not members. The members range from the great powers to ministates, but in legal theory and United Nations practice all are sovereign and equal, each entitled to its one equally weighted vote. (This principle, I might remark in passing, has some rather odd consequences. For example, at least twenty-two United Nations members, with twenty-two votes or about 15 percent of the total, are states with a population each of less than 500,000—about half the size of the city of Dallas. On the other hand, five states, with five votes or about 3 percent of the total, contribute over 60 percent of the United Nations budget.)

Small or large, all of these states have citizens and

all have governments. All have relations with the citizens and governments of other states. These interrelations across national boundaries—of citizens with other citizens, of governments with other governments, of citizens with governments other than their own—are of vital concern to all of us. So also of concern must be the law which regulates these relations—international law in the broadest sense, or, as Judge Philip Jessup has christened it, "transnational law." And this brings me to the main purpose of these remarks: To set out—necessarily in rather summary form—one person's view of that body of law and where it stands today.

Let me deal first with an initial question which is often asked as we look out on a world which seems again and again to be in disarray: Is there any such thing as international law?

To answer, I must first ask you what you mean by "law," for law is a word of many meanings. If you find law only in the command of a political superior, or only in a rule which can be enforced by a policeman, you may find it easy to conclude that international law is no more than a standard of morality or a code of convenience—a code which may lubricate the conduct of international relations but does not govern it. I would suggest, however, that so narrow and formalistic a view of law fails to account adequately for many of the observed facts of legal life, both domestic and international. Is it not more accurate to view law as an instrument of social control within a community, based on principles which are generally accepted as authoritative and which promote the common interest of any community in justice, peace, and good order? On such a view as this, domestic and international law are both "law," seeking the same ends in many of the same ways.

This view is in fact confirmed by the universal practice of states, which habitually acknowledge the existence of international law and constantly assert the legal character of the rights and duties which flow from it. Yet the skepticism with which international law is often viewed perhaps calls for a few further words on two points of difficulty which are often seen as stumbling blocks to its recognition as a binding legal system. The first of these turns on the doctrine of the sovereignty of the national state and asks how it is possible for states sovereign by definition to be subjected to a superior law. The second emphasizes the lack of effective sanctions in the international sphere and asks how any system so weak in means of coercion can be regarded as law.

Discussions of sovereignty, like discussions of other mystical concepts, all too easily become mere intellectual juggling which offers no real enlightenment. For example, if sovereignty is held to mean power unfettered by any restraint except the state's own will, the state can be bound by international law only insofar as it consents thereto. But this consent means nothing even if given, for the state in the exercise of its absolute power can revoke its consent at its pleasure. On the other hand, it can be said with equal logic that if a state cannot give irrevocable consent to be bound, then there is something it cannot do and this contradicts the basic assumption that it can do whatever it wills. The absurd results to which such views lead obviously have no relation to reality, and we are reminded once again of Justice Holmes's admonition that the life of the law has been not logic but experience.

The difficulty disappears if international law is seen as the "necessary concomitant"—in the words of Sir Cecil Hurst—of relations in a world of national states. With the establishment in the world of political entities which are independent but which must carry on intercourse with one another, international law in some form begins to emerge—not because of any conscious will or consent by the participants, but simply as a result of circumstances, of the need for order in their mutual relations. On this approach, sovereignty is no longer a "metaphysical concept" but "merely a term which designates an aggregate of particular and very extensive claims that states habitually make for themselves in their relations with other states." (J. L. Brierly, *The Law of Nations* (5th ed.), p. 48.) Because these claims are large, they at times present serious obstacles to the efficient functioning of international law. But the problem in these terms is no longer the metaphysical one of whether states possess "absolute power," but the practical one of how law can increase its effective control over entities which possess power and assert a wide freedom to use it. This leads to the second of the two objections I mentioned, the question of sanctions and enforcement.

The problem of how to make law fully effective with respect to groups which possess power is one, I would emphasize, which exists in every legal order. Even within a modern state, with its array of sophisticated legal institutions, it is one thing to compel

one or a few individuals by force to comply with the
law. It is something else again to compel large or
well-organized groups, particularly if strongly held
values are at stake. The capacity of law for effective
coercion decreases as the groups involved increase
in strength and influence. For an example of this
process at work, one need look no further than Poland; and for its ultimate result if unchecked, one
need look only to contemporary Lebanon. The point
of the lesson is that in the long run the effectiveness
of law in any society depends less on the powers of
coercion at its disposal than on a general public acceptance of the law as an essential and respected
element of orderly social existence. Only when such
a general acceptance—or at least acquiescence—
provides a foundation, is it possible to invoke coercion successfully in particular instances.

Pressures of the same kind operate also in international law. The national states which constitute the
power groups in the international community tend
by nature to be insistent on their prerogatives and
difficult to subject to the discipline of law. More than
domestic law, therefore, international law depends
on a high degree of acceptance—or, again, at least
acquiescence—among states to make its rules effective in practice. In some areas of its concern, this
consensus is substantial, just as it normally is within
national communities. In such cases a degree of effectiveness results which compares favorably with
that reached by many national legal systems. But in
other areas there is uncertainty and controversy, and
in still others the law has yet to make its entry.

As views diverge, the common basis of acceptance shrinks and effectiveness diminishes. Because states claim for themselves a general right to interpret what the law requires of them and are often reluctant to submit to the binding decision of an impartial tribunal, conflicting opinions may be maintained for a long time before a rule is settled. Even then, acceptance may not be universal, and in such circumstances the precise content of the law may long remain obscure. Yet, once more I would remind you that obscurity and prolonged uncertainty are not traits confined to international law; national legal systems also have their full share of such gray areas.

The shortcomings of international law are real and regrettable, but the fault lies less in the law than in ourselves. As with legislation at home, we get for the most part what we are willing to accept. Yet after all the gaps and failures are noted, there still remains a concept of international law which is valid and enduring. Its vitality is attested by the very cries of outrage which arise when it is seen to fall short, and by the ways in which its requirements are vindicated, often years later. Let me give one example, not too far from here. In 1911 an arbitral commission awarded to Mexico a disputed tract of land—the Chamizal tract—on the Mexican-United States boundary in the Rio Grande River near El Paso. For various and not wholly convincing reasons, the United States refused to accept the award as valid and binding, and the matter remained a sore point in its relations with Mexico for over fifty year. But in 1963 the two countries concluded a treaty finally giving effect to the award and acknowledging by implication the legal duty to honor the decision.

Thus far we have been considering the nature of international law and the problems involved in assuring its effectiveness. These problems are perennial; they have been with us since the days of Grotius and before, and will continue to be throughout the foreseeable future. But the world is not static. New problems appear before we have solved the old ones, and law must respond somehow to a whole range of new developments. In recent years, particularly since the end of World War II, every legal system has been faced with unprecedented challenges, and international law is no exception. Let us look now at some of these changes, and the responses to them which international law is generating.

The problems come for all directions. The most conspicuous, perhaps, arise from the new frontiers opened up by science and technology. Here is a random selection of examples, to which one can easily add others. One could list the problem of outer space and of a regime for the moon and other bodies, natural and artificial; the management of communication and broadcasting satellites, which are no respecters of old-fashioned national boundaries; the new hazards of environmental pollution, again no respecter of boundaries; weather modification; the new uses of the oceans and their resources; and so on and so on.

Other pressures on the law spring from economic and social causes, most notably the accelerated worldwide demand for improved living standards amid the "revolution of rising expectations." This in turn involves demands for the necessary capital investment, most of which must flow across national boundaries, and raises the corollary need for a legal regime which will ensure the requisite stability and security. Related to these is still another group of challenges which have their roots in a heightened sense of international moral responsibility for the dignity and welfare of individual human beings. This urge is already bearing fruit—imperfectly, erratically, yet nonetheless clearly—in the growing measure of protection afforded by international law to fundamental human rights.

In assessing the legal responses to such challenges as these, one must not forget the constraints imposed by the realities of contemporary world politics. In particular, the conflicts between East and West and the North-South tensions between developed and developing countries set limits to the areas of consensus within which new legal approaches can expect to find support. Yet, despite these stresses, it is striking to observe how much progress has in fact been made. Violent rhetoric, and sometimes violence itself, may seize the headlines; but in many fields there has been a remarkable and relatively unnoticed growth in practical international legal arrangements. It is a phenomenon worth a brief review.

Taking note of some of the problems already mentioned, we can observe that the framework of a regime for outer space has been in place since 1967. By the terms of a multilateral treaty signed that year, to which some eighty states are now parties (including all the technologically advanced countries), the exploration and use of outer space, "including the moon and other celestial bodies," is declared to be "the province of mankind," open to all. It is not subject to national appropriation, and the placing of nuclear weapons in orbit around the earth or in outer space is prohibited. Subsequent agreements—relating to the rescue and return of astronauts, to registration of objects launched into space, and to liability for damage caused by space objects—have since been brought into force. For all these instruments, the rate of general acceptance is high and there appears to be a wide measure of consensus on the basic principles. Even allowing for the fact that only a few of the states parties possess space capabilities of their own, and hence there was little reason for them to disagree, the legal response is, I suggest, an encouraging one.

The detailed regulation of satellite communications is an extraordinarily complex technical matter which falls within the purview of the International Telecommunications Union, a specialized agency of the United Nations. At present, substantial controversy exists with regard to satellites in geostationary orbits over the equator. These satellites, which rotate with the earth and hence maintain a relatively fixed position above the earth's surface, are the most desirable for efficient mass communications, but both the number of suitable positions and the number of suitable radio frequencies are limited. How to maximize use of the available resources is the subject of much scientific argument and is yet unresolved; but a conference is to convene, I understand, in 1984 to deal with these technical problems. This is promising, but the situation has been further complicated by recent claims of some equatorial countries to sovereignty over the space above their territories and hence to control over any satellites placed there. The whole situation well illustrates the variety of problems which a scientific advance can engender and with which the law must eventually deal.

The recent developments which I think are most interesting from the standpoint of our present discussion relate to the law of the sea. That law, built up mostly in the days when the only important uses of the oceans were for navigation and fishing, was long one of the most settled elements in the corpus of international law. Those uses still remain the most important today; but their expansion, coupled with the addition of new uses and new concerns, was creating situations by the 1950s and 1960s with which the traditional rules were wholly inadequate to cope. Once again technology—that genie that will not stay in its bottle—has been the chief culprit. Not only did it make commercial fishing so efficient as to endanger many fish stocks, it also brought hitherto inaccessible resources within reach—first petroleum and gas on the continental shelves, then mineral resources in and under the deep sea.

Along with these developments, pressures mounted from coastal states anxious to control all resources off their shores for a substantial distance seaward, generally 200 miles. At the same time, the bloc of developing countries in the United Nations—the so-called "Group of 77"—sought an international regime for resources in ocean areas beyond the limits of national jurisdiction which would favor their interests and forestall possible acquisition by technologically advanced countries on a first-come basis. All these forces combined to make a comprehensive recasting of the older law imperative.

The upshot was the convening by the United Nations in 1972 of a Conference on the Law of the Sea, after several years of preliminary skirmishing. The Conference completed its work, in the form of a single new multilateral Convention on the Law of the Sea, in 1982. It is impossible here to go into the substance of this massive document, which comprises 320 articles and nine annexes. Suffice it to say that it is in effect a constitution for ocean space, dealing with almost every aspect of the uses mankind makes of this 70 percent of the earth's surface: navigation by sea and air; control of living and non-living resources; the rights of coastal states, of sea-faring states, of landlocked states; the regimes of the territorial sea, of straits, of archipelagoes, of exclusive economic zones, of the continential shelf, and of the high seas; marine pollution; marine scientific research; and the settlement of disputes.

The most interesting point about the Conference is that it was able to produce any convention at all. Unlike some of the other subjects I have mentioned, everyone has a stake in the law of the sea in one way or another—even Mongolia, the most landlocked state on earth, which took part in the Conference and has signed the Convention. Issues of vital importance to many states were involved—control over valuable resources, freedom of navigation and commerce, protection of national security, even access to the sea. The extraordinary thing about the Conference is that it was able to work out answers to most of these problems which were acceptable to the great majority of the participants.

The process was not an easy one. It took ten years for the some 150 states which participated to produce the final text. The Conference was the longest, most complex, and most comprehensive international negotiation ever held. At times it was on the brink of collapse, but somehow each time it survived. Much of its eventual success was due to the patience and skill of a number of individuals whose imaginative mediation in the role of honest brokers again and again brought forth acceptable compromises in what was one of the greatest horse-trading meetings in history. It is worth noting that some of the best of these individuals came from the smaller states— Norway, Sri Lanka, Fiji, Singapore, and Venezuela, among others. The proof of their accomplishment came in the final vote on adopting the text, which was approved by the Conference by a count of 130 in favor to four opposed, with seventeen abstentions. The Convention is now open for signature and ratification—over 120 states have already signed— and by its terms it is to come into force after sixty ratifications have been received.

Is the Convention as written a good thing or not? The present administration in Washington thinks not. The United States was one of the four states to vote against the text and has declared that it will not sign the treaty or take part in the preparatory work for its implementation. This is a marked change of policy from the three prior administrations, under all of which the United States took a leading part in the negotiations, originated many of the concepts adopted, and was represented by a series of extremely able delegates. The reason given is dissatisfaction with the Convention provisions on deep-sea mining, which are claimed to be unfair to American interests and hostile to American beliefs in private enterprise and free markets.

For my own part, I believe the advantages of the Convention substantially outweigh the disadvantages. It is, of course, an intricately interwoven series of compromises, in which no one got everything but everyone got something. On the good side, it establishes uniform rules and guidelines on many matters hitherto unsettled, including many of great value to the United States. Among other things, it contains the most comprehensive provisions for dispute settlement yet framed in any treaty and makes resort to them mandatory in most instances. On the bad side, I have to agree that the regime for deep-sea mining is far from ideal. It is unwieldy, burdensome, bureaucratically top-heavy, and probably capable of being tilted against developed countries with free-market economies. Yet it is only one part of a very large treaty whose advantages may not be available to the United States as a nonparty. The decision not to sign for the reasons given seems to me a case of the deep-sea mining tail wagging the Convention dog, and I consider it an error we may come to regret.

I have dwelt on the Law of the Sea Convention at some length partly because I am especially familiar with it, but also because it is a remarkable *tour de force* in international lawmaking. That so many states had the stamina and will to work out an agreement affecting so many issues of direct consequence to them is a notable accomplishment—perhaps the most notable yet achieved in modern international law. The fact that it could be done, and done on the whole pretty well, is, I suggest, a good omen for the future development of international law.

The examples I have cited so far have been responses to challenges originating chiefly in new scientific advances. Before summing up, let me refer briefly to some legal responses to recent concerns arising from other causes.

The growth in international trade and investment since World War II has, of course, been phenomenal, and has been accompanied by a parallel growth in legal mechanisms to facilitate such activities. Among other developments, one may note the increasing use of international commercial arbitration as a method of dispute settlement. The institutions for such arbitration—the International Chamber of Commerce, the American Arbitration Association, and the Stockholm Chamber of Commerce for East-West arbitrations in particular—have never been busier. Further, their activities have been much strengthened by such measures as the Convention on the Recognition and Enforcement of Foreign Arbitral Awards and by the legislative trend in many countries toward freeing transnational arbitration proceedings from local impediments. Also to be noted is the marked movement toward unification of the legal rules governing international trade, evidenced most recently by the new Convention on the International Sale of Goods. And with respect to governments particularly, the increase in commercial trading by states themselves or their agencies has led in several countries (including the United States) to a more restricted view of the immunity from jurisdiction enjoyed by foreign governments and to greater subjection of their commercial activities to the ordinary law.

These developments have on the whole been beneficial. But on the other hand it must be observed that during this same period there has been a vociferous tendency on the part of some states to assert over foreign investment within their territories an almost unlimited power of expropriation, with compensation (if any) to be determined solely at the discretion of the taking state. This attitude, prominently expressed in United Nations debates and resolutions of the 1970s, was also reflected in a number of questionable expropriations at that time.

But even here the picture is not as dark as it may have seemed some years ago, and there are two particularly encouraging signs. One is the fact that in several recent instances of takings substantial compensation has in fact been ultimately paid despite prior oratorical posturings. Thus Libya, in three cases involving the expropriation of oil concessions without payment, refused to take part in subsequent arbitral proceedings; yet in each instance, after awards of varying import were handed down, compensation in agreed amounts was paid quietly and almost *sub rosa*. The other promising sign has been the notable increase in bilateral investment protection treaties between developed and developing countries. Some 150 of these are now in existence, and it may well be contended that this protection of foreign investment in practice is legally much more significant than the adverse rhetoric in the United Nations General Assembly.

My last examples of progress in the development and application of international law relate to the increased recognition on the international plane of individual human rights. Do not misunderstand me. I am well aware that in many quarters of the world such rights are still systematically and brutally violated and that little or nothing has been, or indeed could be, done about it. But other developments stand in contrast to those grim facts. On the level of legal principle, there is now broad support for the view that human rights, even as between a state and its own citizens, are a proper and important concern of international law. This sentiment is embodied in the Charter of Human Rights and the subsequent Convention on Human Rights, as well as in other international instruments now in existence. The practical significance of these efforts may be limited, but their symbolic significance, as expressions of moral values common to all mankind, should not be undervalued. And beyond these there have been important practical measures taken in recent years, most notably in the establishment of the European Commission on Human Rights and the European Court of Human Rights and, more recently, the establishment of the similar Inter-American Commission and Court. These institutions deal or can deal with actual cases, and from their work is emerging gradually a body of law which should be a major contribution to the improved international protection of the fundamental rights of individuals.

In these remarks I have sought to sketch—broadly and perforce incompletely—one view of how international law works and where it stands today. I have suggested that international law exists because there is an inescapable need for it in a world of separate states—a need which is becoming more pressing as transnational relations between governments and peoples proliferate and grow more intricate. The effectiveness of that law rests, as it does ultimately in all legal systems, on acceptance by its subjects. Where acceptance is widespread, in new areas of concern as well as in old, effectiveness is high.

Yet major areas of transnational relations still exist which are governed by policy rather than by law. These will remain until it can be demonstrated that the true interests of governments and peoples will be better served by law than by policy. International law is progressing in some of these areas, as recent developments show, but it still has many miles to go. In the meantime, I submit, our task is to continue to revise and improve it, to demonstrate in practice that it can be fashioned to meet the basic human needs for justice, peace, and order. It is a task for all of us, for no man is an island, and we are all involved in mankind.